SWEDISH
antiques

TRADITIONAL FURNITURE AND
OBJETS D'ART IN MODERN SETTINGS

KARIN LASEROW

BRITT BERG

PHOTOGRAPHY BY NIKLAS LUNDSTRÖM

SKYHORSE PUBLISHING

With thanks to Dennis Anderson and Emma Höglind, Margaretha Bessfelt, Charlotta Bond and Peder Lamm, Galleri GKM, Agneta Gynning, Bodil Lachmann, Agnetha and Paul Larsson, Moderna Möbelklassiker, Olson & Gerthel, and Maria Schad.

CONTENTS

Having worked with antiques for over thirty years now, my ambition, my vision, has always been to unite the past with the present. Antiques are not dusty, historical objects that only belong in castles and country houses or in old surroundings. Quite the contrary. Whether you live in the big city in an ultra-modern apartment, or have just moved into your first home, or if you have a house in the country, or have small children—antiques fit in anywhere and everywhere. When older objects are combined with modern design and architecture in the right way, it creates a dynamic atmosphere that is pleasant to live in. That is how I want antiques to be used—in every possible setting, without exaggerated respect. It is only then that the fantastic craftsmanship of the past becomes alive in the present, and has the chance to live on into the future.

For a long time I have wanted to write a book with a focus on antiques— the history of their styles, dates, and origins—which at the same time shows them in the company of modern furniture and in new, unexpected settings. Now, at last, it is finished. This book takes you on a gentle journey through history's stylistic eras, but also gives concrete and practical advice on how to use antiques today. With the help of beautiful photographs, I want to show how antiques and modern interiors can combine to create harmony and balance. I hope that you the reader will be inspired to include vintage objects and antiques in your home and your everyday life.

Older pieces do not have to cost a fortune. Neither do they need to be in prime condition to bring pleasure. You can enjoy an antique despite flaws and repairs. Last, but not least, there are so many new uses for antiques. All you have to do is dare.

Welcome to my world!

Karin Laserow

English wingback armchair covered in patinated leather. The brass tacks highlight the curves of the armchair's contours.

Old and new together make for exciting combinations. Here the modern cut-glass candlesticks contrast beautifully with candlesticks from the nineteenth century.

Old and new
can enrich each other

For most of us, home is one of the most significant factors in our lives. Home is where you retreat in order to relax and recharge. Home is where you get together with family and friends. And in an age when new interior design trends come thick and fast, it is important to remember that as long as your home fulfills your own needs and reflects the kind of person you are, there is no right or wrong in how you furnish and decorate it. Pink, black, or white; minimalist, modernist; clutter-lover or antiques nerd: It makes no difference. The important thing is to feel that your home is a reflection of yourself, a place of harmonious contentment.

The significance of the home is not a modern phenomenon. From a historical perspective it has always been a cherished priority, as the English lawyer Sir Edward Coke (1552–1634) put it when he wrote "My home is my castle"—a classic quote which is still much used today.

If you look closely, not as much as you might think has changed since the first furniture was made. Instead, what you will see is mostly a rejuvenation of forms and design elements that are many hundreds of years old. It is the materials and construction techniques that have changed: The craftsmen of the past lacked the technical and manufacturing possibilities we have today, and our freedom to use stainless steel, plastics, and other materials. We have a greater range of choice than our forefathers ever had, which is why we can upholster a baroque chair in vinyl, should we choose to. When it comes to furniture and interior design, there are no clear-cut, binding relationships between the past and the present. Old and new can enrich each other. History and our own time are not each other's opposites. That is why a mixture of new materials and old forms can work so well together with beautifully aged antiques.

A Swedish Empire style mirror from the beginning of the nineteenth century could be placed to good effect in a hall, bedroom, or living room to give a sense of greater space.

An antique's charm
has nothing to do with its price.

How to achieve a harmonious balance between antique and modern when decorating your home? Are there any golden rules? Not really, but there are some simple guidelines that will make your life easier. The first is to take a good look at the context in which the antique will be used, so that it has a chance to blend in. It is also important not to stare blindly at monetary value, rejecting things that are "too cheap." Nothing is beautiful just because it is expensive; an antique's charm has nothing to do with its price. A simple wooden piece that costs a few dollars can have the same effect as an expensive chest of drawers.

From a purely practical point of view, it is best to begin by choosing large pieces or items of furniture before moving on to the smaller objects. When properly placed, tall and low furniture can work well together. The primary purpose of seating furniture is to create a variety of comfort zones. Where is it pleasant to sit? Try out different places around your home. Perhaps at the fireside, if you have one. Or by a window with a favorite view. A room can have more than one comfort zone. New upholstery on a Late Empire mahogany armchair from the Swedish Karl Johan period combined with a delicate glass-topped table creates an inviting impression. An ottoman can serve as a footstool or a perch for a tea set. If you want to add some extra color to your life, re-cover a painted Gustavian ottoman with orange or lilac velvet.

Lighting of various kinds and from different epochs is a mood-setter in any decoration scheme. When you want to create a cozy atmosphere, the glow of a candelabra is unbeatable, whether it is placed on a kitchen table or the edge of a bathtub, and there is very little that can truly compete with the beauty of the dancing light from a Gustavian crystal chandelier above a dining table. Lighting effects can be reinforced by well-placed mirrors that reflect and enhance the light in a room. However, mirrors have an even more important function: they extend any room and convey a sense of space.

Le Corbusier's chaise longue in black leather from the mid-twentieth century, an excellent example of an old idiom expressed in a new material. Behind it, an eighteenth-century religious painting. These types of paintings are often underrated, despite their high quality and decorative value.

A home should stimulate all the senses

The last phase in furnishing a home is choosing those all-important ornaments. There are often a multitude of surfaces that can be used for arranging various objects. Instead of setting out things singly, it is far more restful for the eye to group them into different still-life arrangements. A still life can consist of a memento of childhood together with a designer glass bowl, or a yard-sale bargain placed with framed photographs of your nearest and dearest. You can create an impressive effect by grouping together a variety of candlesticks in different materials and of differing types to make an exciting collection.

However, antique objects in modern settings are not merely a question of decoration. There is also the way they build bridges between furniture of different eras and styles. In our evermore borderless, globalized world, there is a risk that invaluable local cultural heritage will become lost. When you choose to put antique furniture and objects into a contemporary setting, cultural heritage is perhaps not foremost in your mind, but nevertheless it is a choice that helps to keep alive the culture embodied by older furniture—an eloquent way to preserve the artistic values and the craftsmanship that it represents.

Finally, a home should stimulate all the senses. The eye should draw pleasure from colors you love and things you like. Scents should be pleasing—perhaps a lovely bouquet of lilies in a Ming vase, or dried lavender in an antique pewter dish. A smooth velvet sofa or a soft wool throw are pleasurable to the touch. There are many small individual impressions that together contribute to the overall sense of harmony we all want in our homes. The desire for symmetry and balance is innate to us all.

A restrained Gustavian card table in mahogany with brass detailing integrates well into a modern scheme. English candlesticks in silver plate and a colorful vase from Rörstrand.

Sometimes
old furniture
is more modern
than the modern
furniture.

Old furniture can take on a new lease of life.
Here a chest of drawers from the 1950s has
taken on a modern expression with glossy
black paint.

Renaissance

An age of awakening, when the geometric forms of classical
antiquity gave harmony and balance to rooms and interiors.

Sweden and the Renaissance

The Renaissance, which means "rebirth," was a period in furniture history that was influenced by the Roman Catholic church losing its grip on society. In a wider perspective, the Renaissance has been described as a time that saw the rise of individualism, freed from the yoke of the church. It was time for the individual to take a central role and to have a rich and meaningful life.

The Renaissance's stylistic exemplars came from Italy at the start of the fifteenth century, with a strong influence from classical architecture and sculpture. Acanthus leaves, with their deeply cut forms, were used as a decorative motif on furniture and to pattern gilt leather. Soft C-forms, in the so-called auricular style, were also common. In the later fifteenth century, examples of Renaissance ideals in art and design spread to the rest of Europe with the help of engravings. As this was the period that saw the advent of printing, the visual language of the Renaissance was also transmitted through illustrations in bibles and books of architecture.

The church had long been the largest employer of craftsmen and artists. With the Renaissance, that role fell to royal families and their courts. In this way, artists and cabinetmakers were challenged to advance and develop their craft. Dining became an important feature of aristocratic life, and led to the commissioning of furniture and fittings specially intended for feasts and formal dining. Most of all, there was a new interest in creating a total impression of harmony and balance in interior spaces and their decor.

The Renaissance style reached the Nordic countries in the early sixteenth century: In Sweden, the Renaissance is generally reckoned as the period between 1520 and 1650. It was largely immigrant craftsmen who brought the new style with them to Sweden. Craftsmanship, fine carpentry, and cabinetmaking were also spread by itinerant journeymen. A distinct Swedish Renaissance style as such never developed. Instead, in the first decades of the seventeenth century, Swedish craftsmen were inspired by German cabinetry. Holland was another country that influenced the Swedish Renaissance. The German and Dutch models were realized with a Nordic touch, however.

Patinated oak chair, probably of French origin, which in Renaissance times would probably have been fitted with an extra cushion for comfort's sake. The chair is surprisingly comfortable to sit in, despite its age.

In the beginning, Renaissance rooms would have only had a few pieces of furniture of the simplest design and construction.

Gustav Vasa and his sons Eric XIV and John III furnished the castles of Gripsholm and Kalmar in an extravagant and splendid Renaissance style. For the interiors, the court commissioned art and furniture from continental Europe. This was to have an abiding effect on the course of the Swedish Renaissance.

Renaissance rooms would have had only a few pieces of furniture of the simplest design and construction. Initially, the most common form of seating was benches fixed along the walls. However, there were also more cozy seats in bay windows. The first years of the seventeenth century saw the introduction of chairs that were tall, straight, and simple, and often fitted with loose cushions for the back and seat to make them more comfortable. Despite the chairs' simple construction, often in oak, they were regarded as luxury items. During the later part of the period, some chairs began to be manufactured on a larger scale, but as items of furniture it was only during the Baroque that they became common.

Chests were not only the Renaissance's storage furniture; they were also used to sit on. They were usually simple and plain, but there were also exclusive variants, richly decorated with carvings, reliefs, and intarsia. Another piece of furniture used for storage introduced at this time was the cupboard or press, which originated in Germany and Holland. The cabinet, which developed into one of the most magnificent pieces of late Renaissance furniture, contained drawers and secret compartments for things such as writing materials, jewelry, medals, and coins; to make one required a wide range of skills, and they often formed a cabinetmaker's masterpiece—a proof of competence after a five-year apprenticeship and the requisite time as a journeyman or waged craftsman. Those who passed the test and became masters were permitted to set up their own business.

Over the mantelpiece hangs part of a Southern European book-cover from the sixteenth or seventeenth century. It consists of a leather-clad wooden panel, decorated with rivets, surrounded by embossed roundels in geometric patterns. A historic artifact that enhances its modern setting.

Baroque

A period of magnificent style and grandiose forms,
befitting Sweden's time as a great European power. Louis XIV
and his court at Versailles were the guiding example.

Immense dynamism and exaggerated forms

In the history of the art of furniture-making, the Baroque makes up the most extensive period. The word itself comes from the Portuguese for a misshapen, uneven pearl—*barroco*. The style was born in Italy in the sixteenth century as part of a demonstration of power by the Catholic church against the ever greater Protestant influence in Europe. The Baroque style reached its mature expression at the court of Louis XIV, and from there spread widely. By 1650 the style was established in Sweden and the rest of Europe. It pushed aside the Renaissance ideals of harmony and symmetry in preference for grandiose forms and strong colors. In Holland, Britain, and Germany, the Baroque was more restrained and less extravagant in appearance. The century-long Swedish Baroque is usually divided into the Carolean High Baroque (1650–1730) and the Late Baroque (1720–1750), the latter sometimes called for Frederick I of Sweden.

In Sweden, which had become a great power after its successes in the Thirty Years War, the Baroque ideal was welcomed with open arms. Returning soldiers wanted a lifestyle in keeping with the country's new position, and Queen Christina rewarded her aristocratic officers with land and country seats.

Baroque architects, represented in Sweden by Nicodemus Tessin the Older and Jean de la Vallée, rejected the Renaissance castle, with its courtyards, fortifications, and moats, in preference for groups of buildings surrounded by magnificent gardens with fountains, ponds, sculptures, and pavilions, framed with neatly trimmed box hedges. Drottningholm Castle outside Stockholm has one of the best-preserved Baroque gardens in Sweden.

The mansions and country houses of the Carolean period, often with a main building and flanking wings on each side, were timber-built, and are characterized by their functional simplicity. Indoors, rooms were arranged in *enfilade*, with a hall, drawing-room, and bedchambers with their accompanying cabinets, the latter functioning as studies or meeting rooms. Walls were covered with woven tapestries or gilt leather—decorated and embossed calfskin in typical Baroque colors. Printed wallcoverings made of oilcloth or linen were also used. Ceilings were richly decorated with stucco reliefs or plafonds.

During the Baroque the earliest form of storage furniture, the chest or coffer, evolved further into the chest of drawers. Typical features are the curvilinear C and S-forms—volutes—that can be seen most clearly in the top edge and the molding at the bottom of this German oak chest of drawers. This particular chest of drawers, divided into three vertical fields with a matching set of smaller drawers for minor items, has cabriole legs, with their pronounced S-curve.

Magnificent banquets and new pleasures

During the Baroque, the ideal was a rich and opulent lifestyle. Generous hospitality and lavish banquets were important aspects of public life. To give an example, dinner at Queen Christina's court could consist of two services, each of at least twenty dishes.

The Swedish aristocracy adopted novelties such as knives, forks, and spoons in silver and pewter, and silver serving dishes, but European porcelain had not yet established itself in the North. Drinks were usually served in silver jugs or goblets, since glass had to be imported from Italy and Germany and was extremely rare and expensive. Domestic glass began to be produced in larger quantities after the founding in 1676 of one of Sweden's first glassworks at Kungsholm in Stockholm.

Not only festivals and banquets were celebrated in style. During the Baroque, even funerals were expected to be stately and sumptuous. Sometimes there could be a delay over a year while the grieving relatives raised sufficient funds for a fitting funeral.

Baroque fashions in clothing and hairstyles aimed at distinguishing the rich from the poor: Appearance was used to demonstrate a person's status and class. The clothes of the rich were richly embroidered with silver and gold thread, trimmed with pearls and silk ribbons. When Charles X was crowned in 1654, his entire wardrobe was ordered from Paris, including an outfit with 140 diamond buttons. Aristocratic women dressed their hair in elaborate curls supported by metal wire frames and decorated with ribbons and lace, while men wore curled and powdered wigs.

All in all the Baroque was an age of pleasure for society's most well-off, who began to enjoy tobacco and snuff, as well as tea, coffee, and cocoa served from beautiful vessels. The new drinking habits opened up a new trade between East and West: In 1644 as many as sixty thousand Chinese cups were traded through Amsterdam. In the 1740s, Sweden began to import Chinese porcelain direct, following the founding of the Swedish East India Company in 1731.

Engraved glass was introduced in the 1690s, often modeled on glass from Nuremberg. Delicate Kungsholm glass, usually tinted grey or pink, often suffers from so-called glass disease. The crizzling of the surface that gives the glass its milky, scaly appearance, with a network of fine cracks, is caused by an incorrect mix of silicates and alkali oxides in the original glass melt, with a subsequent leaching of alkali salts.

Furniture takes new forms

The Baroque saw the development of freestanding models of furniture that had previously been fixed to the wall, and an entirely new furniture culture was created. In France, the designer and artist Jean Berain the Elder provided an important source of inspiration, and the immigrant German sculptor Burchardt Precht became Sweden's most important cabinetmaker in this period. The architect Nicodemus Tessin the Younger was also responsible for designing furniture and interiors in this new Baroque style.

The visual language of the Baroque varied between the different European countries. France came to represent rich and magnificent decorated furniture, often heavily gilded. In Holland, Britain, and Germany, the style was more bourgeois, showing more restraint in color and form. Characteristic of these three countries were armchairs with spiral-turned legs, or high-backed chairs with shaped and scrolled legs. Sweden took inspiration from both schools, which led to the two main strands in Swedish cabinetry: grandiloquent extravagance and quiet restraint.

The developments in existing furniture during the Baroque resulted in the replacement of storage chests with cabinets, cupboards, and side cabinets for storing personal effects. Side cabinets were smaller cupboards or chests that could be moved about when needed, and were often fitted with handles for that purpose. Benches fixed along the walls were abandoned for freestanding settees, stools, and tabourets. Tables became more common. Often they took the form of folding tables with three legs and a hinged top, or gate-legged tables with two drop leaves. Console tables and writing tables also made their appearance during the Baroque. Typical period details used to enhance the look of a room were mirrors, paintings, and various types of clock, such as long-case clocks, table clocks, and wall clocks. Chandeliers, candlesticks, wall sconces, and girandoles provided lighting.

Textiles in the form of curtains were introduced into drawing rooms. Carpets, which in Swedish were called "floor tapestries," were less common. In the bedchambers, beds were placed with their headboards against the wall and their feet out in the room. Their simple, free-standing wooden frames were decorated with splendid textiles to make a canopy and curtains; when it came to the craftsmanship of Baroque beds, the textiles were regarded as more important than the joinery. The curtains had different functions depending on the season. In winter they were pulled to and helped to keep out the cold. In summer their job was to shut out strong sunlight.

Cupboard from western Sweden dating from the first decade of the eighteenth century with alder-root veneer with characteristic pear-shaped ball feet. Its upper and lower halves can be separated. When it came to storage furniture, cupboards were in competition with chests.

The shield-like keyhole plate
with its coronet was proof of
the owner's high status.

Period details

The western Swedish cupboard on the previous page has several interesting details that are typical of the Baroque. The frame and panels are pine, which was the most usual base for veneers and marquetry. In this case, alder root has been cut into thin slices and laid on the pine panels to form patterns, and then polished. The other most common wood used for inlay during the late Baroque was walnut—an influence from Britain.

The brass keyhole plates shaped like shields with a coronet above are evidence of the owner's high status in society. The cabinetmaker would order the brass fittings from specialist metalworkers, often buckle-makers. The buckle-makers also made the drop-shaped handles or drawer pulls. It is important for the monetary value of a piece of furniture that the metal fittings should be of the same period as the cabinetry.

The hand-forged spring-bolt lock, a sprung lock with a curved outline, demanded great skill from the locksmith so the handmade key would mate perfectly with the bolt.

HOMAGE TO A TYPEFACE

A PHILOSOPHY OF INTERIOR

Meningsfulla saker att samla på

REINVENTING L

SCANDINAVIAN DESIGN SEV

Detaljer

StyleCity NEW YORK

RETHINK

pattern

Swedish secretaire in oak that has been given a dark finish and fitted with drawer pulls and keyhole plates in bronze. Behind the flap is an arrangement of pigeonholes and drawers. On the secretaire stands a bronze sculpture, a stainless-steel bowl from Georg Jensen, and a modern desk lamp with a halogen bulb. The painting has a frame with silvery, laciniated acanthus leaves.

The back of a Swedish
Carolean chair with
English influences.
The crest rail of the
chair with its nested
C-shapes is a typical
Baroque flourish.

The development of the Baroque chair

During the Baroque, demand for seating increased and chair manufacturing gathered pace. In terms of design, the differences between the early Carolean models and those of the Late Baroque are obvious.

The earliest Carolean chairs were derived from simpler Renaissance models, with the acanthus leaf as the favorite decorative motif. They were usually made in birch, oak, or pine, often stained to look like the more desirable walnut. Influences from Britain and Holland led to changes in the Carolean chair, in terms of both its construction and its appearance. The splat became high and narrow, and the crest was decorated with a coronet to symbolize rank, or with S and C-curves, so-called volutes. The woven cane back and seat are an English influence.

The Late Baroque chair, which appeared in Sweden in the first half of the eighteenth century, had in its earliest form an open back with an unupholstered, baluster-shaped splat with a keyhole at the top. The cushioned seat was fixed, or rested on a narrow beading on the inside of the frame. The seat could be covered in cotton, linen, or leather. During the Late Baroque, chairs were usually painted in the subdued colors typical of the era, but they have often been painted over many times since. The shaped front legs, so-called cabriole legs, curve out from the frame in an S-shape. Lower down is a turned H-stretcher which stabilizes the chair and serves as a footrest. The earliest chairs in this style had the most pronounced cabriole legs, a form which softened as the Rococo approached.

Polished oak chair from the early Baroque with Renaissance features. Cushioned seat in gilt leather—leather that has been embossed and painted.

High-backed, gilt-leather-clad Carolean chair with English influences. The crest of the splat and the front of the apron are in the form of a shell. Volute front legs terminate in lion's paw feet. Turned back legs and stiles.

English-influenced Carolean chair in dark-stained oak, recently upholstered in black velvet. The pierced volutes of the front frame harmonize with the crest of the chair splat.

The century of the Baroque chair

Baroque chairs come in many different types and vary greatly in appearance. Embossed gilt leather, in its simplest form just calfskin, but also with relief patterns in gold, silver, and applied color, quickly became the highest fashion for furniture and wallcoverings. Swedish chair-makers were inspired by foreign models. Swedish chairs were commonly made from oak, birch, or pine. In England, walnut was preferred.

Oak armchair from the early Baroque with S-shaped arms. The generous splat and seat have been clad with black velvet at a later date, framed with flower-shaped furniture tacks.

During the transition from the Carolean period to the Late Baroque, chairs were fitted with S-shaped front legs, carved shell motifs on the splat, and a crossbow-shaped apron. Velvet and tapestry were popular upholstery materials.

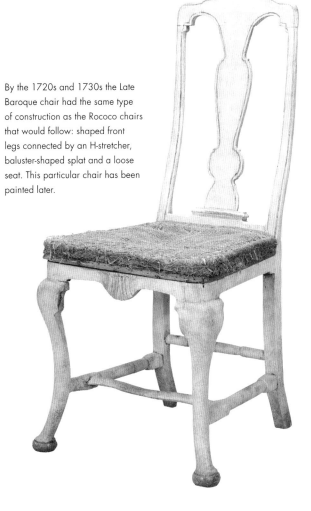

By the 1720s and 1730s the Late Baroque chair had the same type of construction as the Rococo chairs that would follow: shaped front legs connected by an H-stretcher, baluster-shaped splat and a loose seat. This particular chair has been painted later.

Writing-tables with drawers were introduced in around 1700. This alder-root-veneered *bureau à gradin* has two tiers of pigeonholes with smaller drawers. In the kneehole there is extra storage space behind a small door. The baluster feet are typical for the period.

A pine gate-leg table with its original red-brown coloring, with connecting stretchers between the legs and a drawer in the main apron. The tabletop is attached with visible, hand-forged rivets.

New tables for new lifestyles

During the Baroque period, new lifestyles came to demand new types of table tailored to specific purposes. Writing desks with flanking sets of drawers were one of the novel types of furniture that developed. The Swedish dining table was often made of pine and very simple in form—it was made more exclusive by covering it with a beautiful textile such as an oriental carpet.

Card-table with a folding top and cabriole legs, inspired by the English Queen Anne style. It has a drawer with a bat-shaped drawer pull in brass.

Folding table in oak with baluster legs. The divided back leg swings out and supports the tabletop when the leaf is raised, a practical solution for when you need more space at the table.

1950s Denmark and eighteenth-century Sweden in elegant accord. Arne Jacobsen's Myran chairs from 1952 and three of Erik Dahlberg's *Suecia Antiqua et Hodierna* engravings from 1716 are a satisfying visual match with the severe black-and-white staircase. The three engravings have been given new frames, decorated with antique letterforms. Erik Dahlberg's monumental series of engravings depicting the palaces and stately homes of the day have both historical and architectural value. The engraving on the left is of Axel Oxenstierna, Queen Christina's regent, tutor, and advisor, and one of the most influential people in Swedish economic and political life in the seventeenth century.

In the Baroque period,
the dancing candlelight
was enhanced by reflectors.

Baroque lighting

The lighting in Baroque palaces and stately homes was provided by chandeliers, candlesticks, and girandoles, their candlelight reinforced by reflectors.

Chandelier in bronze with a baluster form and a pierced centre. All its detachable parts are numbered so it can be easily reassembled. The S-shaped arms match the sparsely pierced decorative elements, enhancing the chandelier's airy look. The flowers on the upper part of the fitting serve as reflectors to increase the effect of the candles.

French baluster-shaped **brass candlesticks** with chased decoration and octagonal feet.

Floor-standing candlesticks, or torchères, which first appeared in the Baroque, were in most cases intended to be used in ecclesiastical settings. This volute-shaped pair in stamped brass has ribbed ball feet. The rest of the decoration is made up of patterns of scrolls.

Sconce from southern Europe, carved from wood. The openwork frame surrounding the mirrored glass is decorated with broad-lobed, gilded leaves. The arm is fitted with a hand-forged spike intended to take wax candles.

Wall mirror in the Baroque style from around 1700, with naked baby boys, so-called *putti*, flanking the small oval mirror in the crest.
During the Baroque, mirrors represented wealth, and were placed in the reception rooms used for entertaining.
A mirror's function was to enlarge the room, as well as to enhance the visual effect of the table setting
and the sumptuously dressed guests. The large mirror glass is a recent replacement.

Long-case clocks—the latest thing

The long-case or grandfather clock, which originated in Holland in the middle of the seventeenth century, became popular in Britain before coming to Sweden. The Dutch fitted a wooden case around the pendulum to protect it from draughts and knocks, and made it long enough to contain the weights.

Clock-face with Roman numerals on polished brass. The centre of the face was given a matt look by punching a raster pattern into the metal.

The clockface has a seconds-hand and date hand, and the maker's signature.

Britain's trade with the Chinese left its mark on the decoration. Lacquer "à la chinoise" with a landscape, pagodas, and weeping willows in gold leaf on a black-lacquered background.

The painting on the side is of a stylized flower and leaves of the European pattern.

Long-case clock from Ipswich with a brass clockface.

The round clockface in silver-colored metal plate is surrounded by bronzed tin, decorated with dolphins and urns. There are two winding mechanisms—one for striking and one for timekeeping. The clock strikes the half hour once and the hour with the corresponding number of chimes.

The clock is signed Petter Wassberg, who was born in 1738 to a clock-making family from Södermanland.

Long-case clock, scraped back to reveal the original paint. The pendulum's swing can be seen through the small window on the front.

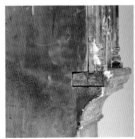

The back of the clock is as important as the front. The genuine patina of the unpainted wood of the back will be decisive for any future treatment.

Swedish long-case clock from the mid eighteenth century by Petter Wassberg.

The moveable cabinet—the filing cabinet of the age—was the most expensive item of furniture in the home, and was used to store things like documents and jewelry. It usually consisted of separable upper and lower parts; the latter now is often missing. This cabinet's surface is of glossy black lacquer with detailing in gold with Chinese motifs. The two doors open to reveal an array of pigeonholes and small drawers, and a centre panel decorated with a Chinese landscape. The drawer fronts, with their small brass knobs, have panels of silver foil embossed with naturalistic plant forms, framed by jacaranda wood and ebony. All the drawers are lined with marbled paper and are discreetly marked with numbers that correspond to numbers on the frame. The cabinet has generously decorated brass mounts.

To have your portrait painted was usually a privilege of the wealth. Many surviving portraits are unsigned; others have the artist's signature or a date on the reverse, known as a signature *à tergo*. Baroque portraits have a greater cultural and monetary value if the frame and the painting are from the same period. This frame has a genuine patina on both the front and the back.

A French **casket** in papier mâché—a mixture of paper and glue—with a leather-clad exterior embossed with geometric patterns. The chased edges of the casket and the handle in the form of a twisted rope are made of brass. Shield-shaped keyhole plate with volute decoration. A **silver** *kåsa*, or quaich, was used for certain kinds of toasts during the Baroque period—the cup might be passed around the whole company, with everyone taking a drink. This silver *kåsa* has oval lobes framed by a punched border and is gilded on the inside. The handle is a grotesque mask of an angel, with a volute frame. **Chinese bowl** in blue-and-white porcelain from the Ming Dynasty (1368–1644). Used as a serving bowl. Four l**eather-bound volumes** of the history of Louis XIV and his age.

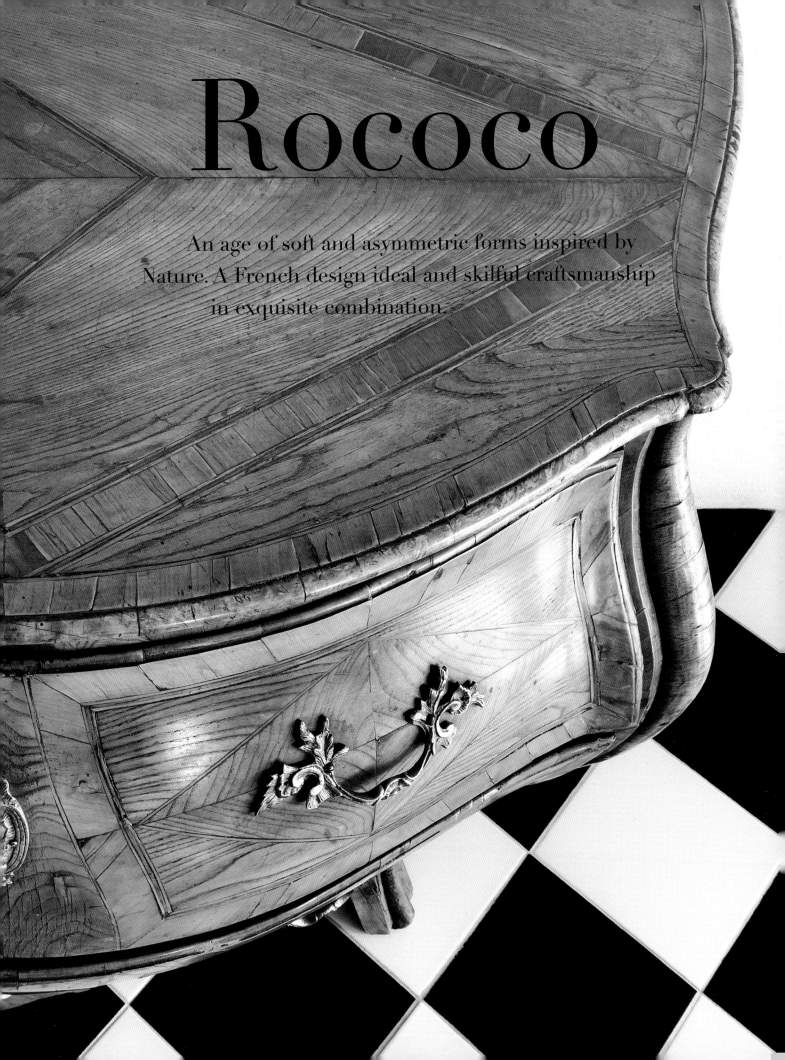

Rococo

An age of soft and asymmetric forms inspired by
Nature. A French design ideal and skilful craftsmanship
in exquisite combination.

Nature as chief source of inspiration

The Rococo period (*c.*1750–1775), in Sweden also called the Age of Liberty, and is perhaps the most playful style in furniture history, filled with life, movement, soft forms, and asymmetry. The style was created by the Italian-born goldsmith Juste-Aurèle Meissonier, whose engravings were to inspire an entire artistic style, *Louis Quinze*, which reached its full flourish in Paris in around 1730. Meissonier was not the only instigator of the Rococo, but he was the most important in international terms.

The ultimate inspiration came from Nature, as idealized by the one of the greatest philosophers of the day—Rousseau. He was hostile to the influence of science and technology on humanity, which he regarded as being far removed from its origins in Nature. Rousseau's conviction that we must find our way back to our roots was not just pervasive among the thinkers of his time, who were passionate about Nature and extolled the joys of a simple, idyllic country life; it had a direct effect on Rococo furniture, with the shell, lifelike flowers, and acanthus leaves, and also exotic figures following Chinese models, becoming its favorite symbols. The Rococo also adopted the motifs of the Baroque, now expressed in a lighter and more charming manner. If the Baroque was masculine in its expression, the Rococo, with its curvilinear visual effects, can be described as more feminine and sensual. Color scales became brighter and lighter than the Baroque's, often using pearl white, rose, yellow, and pale blue, although white in combination with gold was more unusual. The greatest English influence came from the furniture designer and cabinetmaker Thomas Chippendale. In engravings from 1754 it is possible to see his ideas, with their characteristic French Rococo influence, mixed with Gothic elements and Chinese art.

In Sweden, where Linnæus was the great promoter of Nature, the Rococo influenced the design of the new royal palace in Stockholm by the architects Nicodemus Tessin the Younger and Carl Hårleman, both of whom had trained in Paris and Rome. Stockholm Castle had been destroyed in a terrible fire in 1697, but, though work on its replacement began the following year, construction was halted by the Great Northern War, which lasted for over twenty years. It was only in 1723 that building resumed. Tessin designed the palace, but after his death in 1728 his son Carl Gustav Tessin appointed Hårleman

In the soft, curvilinear forms of the Rococo nothing is static. Whether an object is large or small, everything seems to be in a state of perpetual motion. These French candlesticks were made using a technique called *argent haché*: silver-plated brass whose surface is roughened with a steel stylus before being coated with the silver. *Argent haché* was extremely popular during the Rococo, especially in lighting fixtures. The irregularities break up the light and, together with the botanically inspired decoration, give it a radiantly alive look.

as chief surveyor, and gave him the task of finishing construction of the palace. Hårleman was thus responsible for creating the palace's original Rococo interiors.

Two local cabinet-makers of note who contributed to the success of the Rococo style in Sweden were Johan Niclas Eckstein and Carl Petter Dahlström. Both had studied in Paris, and returned with their knowledge and skills to Sweden after completing their training.

Airy salons and tiled stoves

The salons of the Rococo were bright and airy, flooded with light from floor-to-ceiling French windows. Rooms were arranged in *enfilade*, separated by double doors. Walls were divided into sections, filled by woven panels with landscape pictures painted on them in oils, framed by decorative stems of leaves and flowers. Later, landscapes were abandoned in favor of textile panels of silk damask. An important innovation in room design was the use of tiled stoves for heating, invented by the Swedish architect Carl Johan Cronstedt in around 1770. The stoves were a closed source of heat with an internal system of piping and an outer covering of faience tiles—earthenware with a tin glaze—and their much more sparing use of firewood meant they quickly out-competed the older open fireplaces. The tiles were decoratively painted and framed by Rococo details—rocaille motifs, flowering stems, emblems, or figurative scenes.

Of all Rococo furniture, the chest of drawers became the signature piece of the age, with its bulging forms and heavily decorated, fire-gilded drawer pulls and keyhole plates. Styling and intarsia decoration were the main focus for cabinetmakers. The Swedish Rococo chest of drawers usually had a basic structure made of pine, built up from a number of curved segments, roughly two inches thick, which were sawn to shape separately and then glued together. The curved segments were laid horizontally across the apron of the chest of drawers and vertically at the sides. The cabinetmaker used planes, files, and rasps to give the chest of drawers its shape, finishing it with veneers of jacaranda, amaranth, rosewood, walnut, olive, alder root, birch, elm, and other woods. The veneer was hand-sawn and, because of the tools used at the time, it had to be quite thick, 3–5mm.

A chest of drawers was a cabinetmaker's masterpiece. It might be constructed with flanking pillars; it might have straight doors, rounded corners, and shaped legs. The top was rounded and given a curving edge. Chests of drawers were often decorated with intarsia in a checked or diamond pattern.

This corner cupboard, later given a Rococo green color scheme, is an eminently practical piece of storage furniture. It consists of a lower part with a solid door and an upper part set with panes of glass. Both parts together create a well-balanced whole, thanks to such details as the columnar decorations at the sides and the profiles and shapes of the various sections and panels. The soft outline of the cupboard offers three distinct platforms for the display of ornaments.

LIONNI   A COLOR OF HIS OWN

Olof och Lena Landström   NISSES NYA

ANTOINETTE PORTIS

rosenwald and to name but just a

lauren child   I Will Never N

SY

pattern or

Seating was made to be comfortable, with fixed, padded seats of the French model.

Tables had soft contours, with S-shaped aprons and legs. Dining tables were often simple constructions in pine, painted fashionable colors. The most extravagant of the Rococo tables was the console table: made of carved wood, it was then gilded in alternate glossy and matt stripes. The tabletop could be fine stone such as marble, or wood with marbled painting. Seating was made to be comfortable, with fixed, padded seats of the French model. The seats were given generous proportions, reflecting both an increasing appreciation for comfort and to accommodate the immensely wide skirts then in fashion.

Mirrors were rectangular, framed with round corners, and could be fitted with a latticework crest and lower section. Occasionally the mirror glass would be secured in the frame by leading. The decorations of carved and gilded wood took the form of rocailles, volutes, and flowers. Beds were simple in design, with brocade curtains as the only embellishment.

Porcelain and ceramics

The upper classes ate their meals off pewter or silver. In the most exclusive circles, you would find imported Chinese porcelain plates. When the French court of Louis XIV ran into money troubles at the start of the eighteenth century, the royal silverware was sent to be melted down, so the court turned to faience, a tin-glazed earthenware, which began to be produced in Rouen. Faience was a far more pleasant surface to eat from, and soon all of Europe, right down to the lower middle classes, was eating from ceramic plates. French and Swedish faience wares were very similar in appearance, while in Holland, with its extensive trade with China, makers copied Chinese designs.

Europeans greatly admired Chinese porcelain, and tried for many years to discover how it was made. Eventually the Germans succeeded in solving the riddle and the Meissen works began to produce the first European porcelain in 1710. Meissen ware, with its *Deutsche Blumen* decoration, was wildly popular for a number of decades, but the Seven Years War (1756–1763) spelled the end of its dominance as other porcelain factories in Europe took the lead, Sèvres among them. The English began to produce a form of earthenware called creamware, which was considerably cheaper, stronger, and lighter.

Two armchairs in different styles. The chair to the left, upholstered in striped and checked cotton, has carved shells on the apron and arms and acanthus leaves on the legs. The chair to the right has fixed back cushion held in place with tacks and a removable stuffed seat. The blocks are decorated with carved flower details. The floral upholstery harmonizes with the curved back and the other curvilinear forms of the chair. Both chairs have been repainted at a later date.

This Swedish faience plate from
Rörstrand has a curved outer rim
with small ridges, a so-called lobed edge.
The decoration uses the typical blue color
and depicts free-floating flowers.
The Rörstrand porcelain factory was
founded in 1728, and its blue color scale
came to be its signature style. Its main
Swedish competitor, Marieberg, founded
thirty years later, was better known for
its luminous colors.

A plate from the Meissen porcelain factory.
The plate has a curved, volute rim
and is decorated with paintings
of small flowers.

A master cabinetmaker's showpiece

In the Rococo, master cabinetmakers had their best chance to shine when making writing furniture. They could display their professional skill to the full, and often competed with one another in the use of exclusive techniques and materials. The secretaire became one of the age's best-loved pieces of furniture. The French name comes from the Latin *secretus*, meaning separate or hidden, and refers to the array of drawers and compartments secreted behind the lockable front flap.

This desk with its fold-down writing surface can be dated to the mid eighteenth century, to the transition between the Baroque and Rococo styles. The desk's simple lines are Baroque, as are the drop-shaped drawer pulls; the heavily decorated apron and diamond patterns of veneer are typical of the Rococo, as are the handles and keyhole plates of the large drawers and the metal trim between the drawers.

Left: Diamond-veneered drawer fronts with drawer handles and keyhole plates in gilded bronze.
Middle: The secretaire has a hidden compartment at the rear of the right-hand side panel. When the door is closed it is camouflaged by the pattern of the veneer.
Right: The fluted brass trim between the drawer fronts.

The secretaire, with its generous fold-down writing surface, was a practical innovation that first appeared during the Rococo.

The secretaire, with its generous fold-down writing surface, was a practical innovation that first appeared during the Rococo. As it turns out, the flap is also perfect for a laptop computer. This secretaire is typically Rococo. The lower section, which resembles a two-drawer chest of drawers, is topped by a sloping, fold-out writing surface which conceals a series of small, stepped drawers and pigeonholes. The wood is walnut and walnut root, the decorative fittings of fire-gilded bronze.

Left: The writing surface is a practical waxed linen cloth framed by veneer.
Middle: When folded down, the writing flap rests on pull-out supports of forged iron, which terminate in oval brass knobs.
Right: The sabots, or shoes, are pierced rocailles in fire-gilded bronze.

A collection of Rococo furniture in a sitting-room with a blue theme. Between two windows stands a magnificent Swedish Rococo chest of drawers in beautifully patinated pale wood, flanked by two painted French armchairs. The chairs, which have been fitted with extra cushions to bring them up to today's standards of comfort, are upholstered in a combination of plain and patterned blue velvet.

Above: **The lock** is surface-mounted, and thus is visible from the inside. The drawers' shell-shaped **keyhole plates** in gilded bronze are contemporary with the chest of drawers. **The drawers** are constructed with dovetail joints, called "salmoning" in Swedish as the interlocking wood has the shape of a salmon's tail. The sides of the drawer bottom are visible, unlike in later chests of drawers, where the drawer bottom is inset and thus only visible from the back. The S-shaped **corner moldings** are veneered to match the rest of the chest.

Left: The chest of drawers, a masterpiece of craftsmanship, was the favorite piece of furniture in the home. The bulging apron has a veneered central panel in the form of an urn—a typical Swedish feature.

Bowed legs and curvaceous aprons

The Rococo period saw the arrival of many specialized forms of table, including gaming-tables, ladies work tables, tray tables, and dressing tables. Alder root began to be used and drop-leaf tables with round, oval, or square tops and a three-footed pedestal base became popular. The simpler gate-leg table lived on throughout the eighteenth century.

Tray tables were meant for tea-drinking. Like many others of the period, this particular tray table had a water-resistant top made from faience. The faience was both brittle and heavy, and made the table less practical, and many of the original faience tops have either been broken or damaged, or have disappeared. The legs, with their graceful volute form, are decorated with a pattern of carved scales on the "knees," while the apron has a curvilinear form. The paint has been retouched.

Parlor games of various types were one of the pleasures of the well-to-do. This gaming table, with its shaped legs, moldings, and slide-out candlestick stands on the short sides, is just as useful today as in the eighteenth century. The removable top is a chessboard. Playing on an old, patinated chessboard like this one adds an extra dimension to the game. The table has been repainted at a later date.

Historical furniture can be both beautiful and practical in a modern bedroom. Here an English commode serves as a night table. In the past, a chamber pot would have been kept behind the two doors and the lower drawer would have held toiletries. The commode's straight legs have a molding on their outer edge. The patinated trug tabletop has a deep, curved edge. The color of the fur throw echoes the commode's dark tone.

This inviting armchair has a worn armrest whose decoration of acanthus leaves is a survival from the Baroque. A closer look reveals similar decoration at the base of the armrest.

Inspired Rococo chairs

France, England, and Holland took the lead in defining the Rococo chair. French influence showed in soft, shaped cushions, S-shaped legs, and oval, curved seat-backs that were padded and upholstered. There were carved details such as flowers, acanthus leaves, and various shell forms. The English-inspired chairs had a simple basic form and an open back with a baluster splat. The seat was removable and lightly padded. Scalloped carving was common on the apron and the crest of the back.

A French armchair with a typical strengthening bar in the middle of the seat-back. The chair is upholstered in a combination of plain and patterned blue velvet.

A ladder-back "laughing" chair from Lindome in western Sweden, influenced by English models and painted in Venetian red. The name comes from the rungs of the back, which look like two laughing mouths. The chair has elegant proportions, with an oval back, round seat, and molded and shaped legs with floral decoration. The carved flower of the crest is repeated on the middle of the apron.

Armchair with red-and-white-striped cotton covers and a gently curved back, crowned by a carved flower that is repeated on the blockss and in the centre of apron. The soft lines of the chair are accentuated by the raised moldings. For added comfort, the chair has been fitted with an extra cushion.

A French armchair in dark-stained, waxed wood with simple curved forms and molded edges. The checked upholstery and comfortable cushions give an inviting impression. A lively detail is the rear of the seat-back, which has been upholstered using a flower design of Swedish origin.

A powder chair in oak, probably of Norwegian origin. This would have been used to sit on while having your wig powdered. The two shell carvings on the two fronts of the apron are generously proportioned. The straight, fluted legs signal the transition from Rococo to Gustavian.

A Rococo chair from Denmark, as is evident from the sturdy legs and the bronze detailing along the crest rail and the apron. The splat, with its baluster, shows an English influence.

Armchair with gilt-leather seat from the early Rococo in flame birch that has been stained and waxed. The chair's English influences can be seen in the high, open, baluster back, as well as the shaped H-stretcher to brace the legs.

A close-stool in waxed oak, probably from Central Europe. When needed, the gilt-leather seat would have been lifted to reveal the chamber pot underneath—hence the broad apron to hide it.

A hall with an angled wall has been furnished with a practical modern cupboard, setting off a straw-yellow Rococo chair from western Sweden with black leather upholstery. The chair's typical Rococo details include the rocailles on the legs, apron, and crest. A Swedish mirror from the same period completes the picture.

When arranged carefully, ultra-modern pieces fit perfectly with antiques. Here the rectangular dining-table with a polished stone tabletop sets up a dialogue with the English-style Rococo chairs from western Sweden. The chair seats are upholstered in cognac-colored, patinated leather. The play of color between the earthy nuances of the walls and other detailing creates a calm atmosphere. On the table is a piece of traditional Swedish craftsmanship called a *vril*, an entire burl or burr that has been hollowed out to form a bowl—and as beautiful empty as when filled with fruit.

A luxury for the truly wealthy

Mirrors were expensive luxury items, only to be found in the homes of the very rich. They were commissioned from mirror- and frame-makers, whose feeling for design and form resulted in a beautiful pieces of craftsmanship. The mirrored glass was often divided into two sections because large areas of plate glass were difficult to make and attracted a luxury tax.

Left: A large Swedish mirror in gilded and carved wood, intended for a palatial setting. The frame is enhanced by carvings of a woven ribbon and leaf decoration. The crest of the mirror has strongly lobed rocailles that frame a large shield and is topped by a rose, echoed by the rocaille of the volute-formed foot of the mirror. The mirror glass, having been mirror-silvered with mercury on the reverse, has a homogeneous silver color, and is protected by a wooden back panel that has the same patina as the frame, showing it to be original.

Above: A Swedish Rococo mirror that has been taken back to the original gilding. The crest is framed by several C-forms, which at the very top culminate in a rocaille.

Rococo lighting

It was realized very early on that chandeliers with hanging prisms
provided both beautiful and practical lighting for interiors. They were often found
in palaces, stately houses, and the homes of the well-off. French chandeliers were
the models for Swedish craftsmen when the rooms of the Royal Palace
in Stockholm were fitted out.

Above: One Rococo innovation was the wall-mounted light, or wall *applique*, usually of brass or bronze. This one has two curved
arms decorated with leaves.

Right: The Kungsholm chandelier is a pattern that has been enduringly popular in Sweden ever since the Rococo. The name comes
from the Kungsholm glass-works in Stockholm, where the necessary craftsmanship existed to produce clear glass pieces of high
enough quality to be cut and shaped into leaf-shaped prisms. The chandelier's pear-shaped brass framework is hung with facetted
prisms. Where the prisms attach to the frame are flower-shaped glass pieces known as marguerites. The chandelier is bound
together and stabilized with metal wire, which is sheathed in glass tubes to create a cage. The chandelier in the photo was made
towards the end of the nineteenth century and is a high-quality, faithful copy with correct period detailing.

Old and new working together: modern, shocking pink velvet gives a lift to French-inspired Gustavian oval-backed armchairs. When choosing new upholstery the only limits are your taste and daring. Despite its age, the Swedish Rococo pine cupboard is a practical and convenient storage solution. It is easy to move as the top, doors, and upper and lower sections all come apart when needed. The cupboard's typical Rococo touches include the flow of moldings along the top, the shaped legs and the highly decorative front. It has been repainted at a later date.

Pomanders were inconspicuous, but important. Despite the elegance and grace of the salons where aristocratic ladies and gentlemen would have socialized, the smell would have been almost intolerable because personal hygiene was virtually nonexistent. A small sniff of the ammonia mixture in a pomander could help people to put up with the odor. This heart-shaped pomander in silver gilt with its velvety smooth contours is topped by a crown and bears the owner's initials. It is just the right size to sit in the palm of your hand.

An **English silver pot**, with its mid-section worked into a waist to create the Rococo pear shape. Its C-shaped ebony handle, the lid and foot, and the swirling godrooning are all excellent examples of fine silversmith's art. Four **rummers**, or hock-glasses, with engraved bowls, for drinking wine. Rummers could vary in size from 4 to 20 inches. The green color indicates a German or Dutch origin. **Chinese-made sauceboat** from the second half of the eighteenth century, its curved form taken from European models. The pink-dominated color scheme is called *famille rose*. **Plates and beakers in pewter** became more common and were very popular among Sweden's growing middle classes. If silver was too expensive, pewter—"poor man's silver"—was an acceptable alternative as it was good-looking, hardwearing, and easy to keep clean. The rim of the plate is divided into five sections with a molding along the edge. The beaker narrows towards the base, and final outward curl of the foot is a typical Rococo touch.

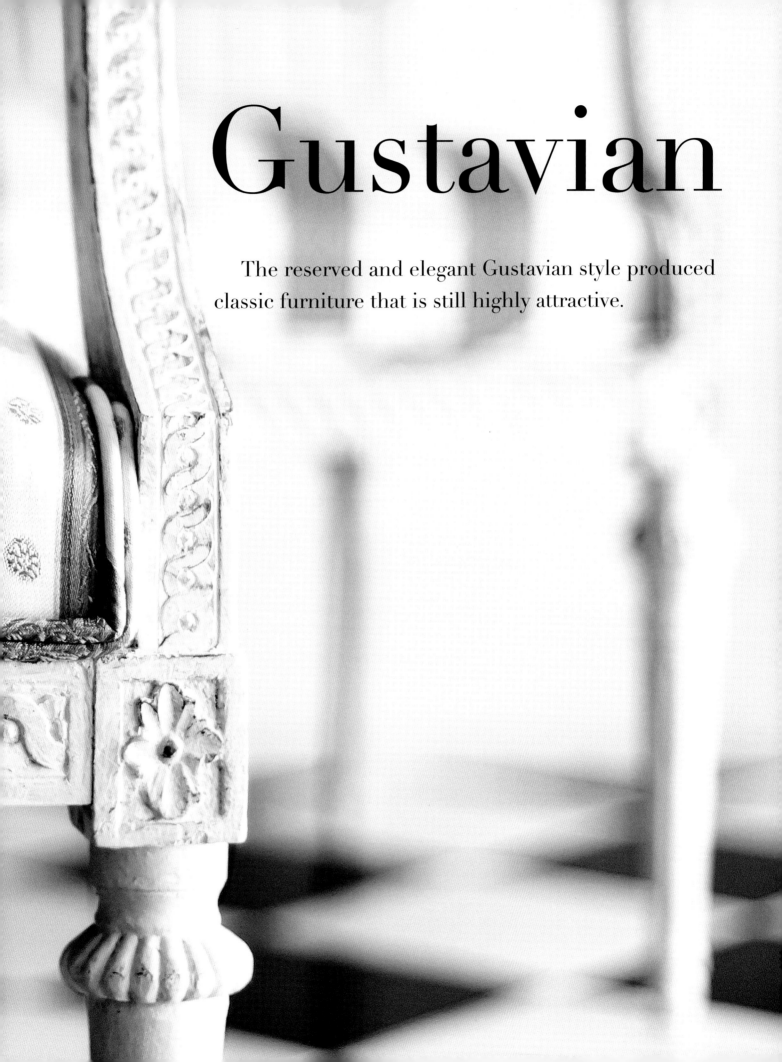

Gustavian

The reserved and elegant Gustavian style produced
classic furniture that is still highly attractive.

Sweden's style king bar none

The Gustavian period, *c.*1775–1810, is regarded as the high point of fine Swedish furniture-making. The great source of inspiration for the style, which first appeared in Paris, were the archaeological discoveries made during the excavations of Pompeii and Herculaneum in the 1730s and 1740s.

In contrast to the Rococo's C- and S-curves and asymmetric shell-like forms, the visual language of the Gustavian period was restrained, with simpler lines and regular, symmetric decoration. In the rest of Europe this reserved furniture style came to be called Louis XVI. Fully developed in France by 1760, there is a clear dividing-line at around 1790 that splits Sweden's Gustavian style into two periods. The initial High Gustavian era is characterized by soft details and mixed forms, while Late Gustavian style after 1790 is consistently austere and regular.

In Sweden the Gustavian era dawned in 1775, thanks largely to King Gustav III, who was crowned in 1771. In Sweden, he was the style's originator and greatest devotee, and his was the name given to the era there. When discussing the Gustavian style, it is important to realize that it refers to the furniture and interior decoration of the homes of the *wealthy*. It was the King and the aristocracy who set the trends for the cultural life of the entire country.

Gustav III was nicknamed "The Theatre King," but should really have been called "The Culture King": He was a passionate and knowledgeable connoisseur who traveled Europe absorbing new influences and creating an extensive network of contacts. When he returned home after his travels, he introduced and supported cultural pursuits such as theatre, opera, sculpture, painting, music, and ballet. He founded the Swedish Academy, modeled on the Académie Française. The Culture King also started the Swedish National Lottery, having been inspired by what he saw in Venice. During Gustav III's reign (1771–1792), Sweden drew closer to the Continent in terms of ideology, politics, culture, and language.

Old meets new. A High Gustavian armchair upholstered in modern striped fabric.

Gustav III was a passionate and knowledgeable connoisseur who traveled Europe absorbing new influences and creating an extensive network of contacts.

It was while visiting Paris that Gustav III came into contact with the new Louis XVI style. When he arrived in the French capital, arrayed in his Rococo finery, he realized that he was hopelessly outdated compared to his French equals. The only thing to do was to swap his entire wardrobe for clothing in the new fashion.

Gustav III instantly took the Louis XVI style to heart, but even so it would take twenty years for the fashion to really establish itself in Sweden. Not that the Swedes were particularly slow adopters; rather, the rapidity of change that we are used to in our modern information society simply did not exist in the eighteenth century. The trend-setters of the day were forced to rely on engravings and drawings that arrived by horse and cart over appalling roads, or by sailing ship.

The architects Jean Eric Rehn and Carl Fredrik Adelcrantz were responsible for bringing the new French style of building to Sweden, having come in contact with it in Paris during the 1750s. Their greatest sources of inspiration were the French court and the royal palaces. Jean Eric Rehn was drawn to the new classical lines and he introduced the style in Sweden's internal and external architecture, as well as in interior decoration and furniture. After Gustav III's journey to Italy in 1783–4, the Gustavian style came to stay in Sweden, with a strong emphasis on models from antiquity.

Despite Gustav III's central place in Swedish cultural history, he was not universally popular in his own day. He ruled at a time when France's royalty and aristocracy faced death as the populace finally revolted against the *ancien régime*. This was a frightening prospect, and was the main reason he staged a coup against Sweden's parliamentary government in the hope of taking power based upon the loyalty of the general population. However, the move only gave him a brief breathing space before fate caught up with him: In 1792 Gustav III was fatally wounded at the Stockholm Opera by a shot fired by Jacob Johan Anckarström.

The Gustavian style lived on in Sweden long after the death of The Theatre King, but without Gustav III at the helm there is no doubt that Sweden lost some of its luster.

The column, which had been the load-bearing element in classical Greek temples, became the Gustavian period's favorite symbol. Here it takes the shape of a cupboard.

Restrained elegance and airy prospects

When it came to interiors, the epitome of Gustavian style was a series of elegant and airy rooms, often separated by double doors decorated with moldings, and crowned with architraves. Walls had painted panels framed by borders made up of classical symbols and patterns, the borders being painted directly onto the wall, or onto linen cloth that was then fixed in place. Ceilings, often whitewashed, were decorated with moldings and stucco. Rooms were lofty, with tall mullion-and-transom windows and floors of pine, oak parquet, or grey limestone.

The classical column was a popular decorative detail, and it came to be the defining element in the Gustavian style. It appeared as pedestals, but also as the bases of girandoles and clocks.

The columnar shape was also echoed in tiled stoves, with their painted borders and patterns of flowers; other stoves were designed to resemble rectangular cupboards, with upper and lower sections. With the advent of the tiled stove, rooms became easier to furnish. Previously, it had been important to group furniture around the open fire for the sake of warmth, but now, thanks to the new form of heating, furniture could be placed freely around the room.

Whatever the scale of the furniture and fittings, they were characterized by the extensive use of perpendicular lines and contours. Other typical details were tapered legs; rosettes in carved wood or as bronze mounts; and urns, often used at the cross-points of table stretchers or on the crests of mirrors, cupboards, and chair-backs. Oval forms were adopted for mirror frames and sconces, chairbacks, or as a crowning decorative element on the tops of objects.

Stripes were the most common pattern for Gustavian textiles, with alternating continuous columns of flowers. Plain stripes and checks were also common. Upholstery was mostly of cotton, except in the homes of the very wealthy, who preferred silk. Typical Swedish column candlesticks.

The Gustavian style was reserved, and beautifully embellished with fine detailing to catch the eye.

Furniture was usually made with a basic structure or frame of pine, which was then decorated with patterns of exotic wood veneers.

The bureau, or chest of drawers, made from expensive woods and with bronze fittings, continued to be the most prized piece of furniture in the home. In terms of quality, gilt furniture was the most exclusive, and was intended for palaces and stately homes. Costly console-tables, often made of carved and gilded wood, are one example. These tables first had molded-edge curved tabletops, but during the Late Gustavian period they took on a rectangular form.

Dining tables in pine were usually very simply made, built as two semicircles or as a drop-leaf table with two flaps that could be folded up and down as needed. Other small tables such as gaming tables, occasional tables, and ladies' work tables had straight, tapered legs. Secretaires or writing tables were the usual Gustavian writing furniture, and these too adopted the new rectilinear style.

Gustavian sofas were mainly of three types: "trough"-shaped; "tub"-shaped; or with a rectangular back and seat. Beds were fitted with high headboards and footboards, usually with carved borders and often a canopy. Just as in earlier periods, the bed-curtains could be drawn around the bed to shut out the sun in summer sun and the cold in winter. The Late Gustavian period saw truckle beds that were pulled out from the long side, rather than from the short end as earlier.

Gustavian mirrors had frames of gilded wood, with decoration in the form of regularly patterned borders. Their crests were often decorated with the popular details typical of the age: an urn, a sheaf, or a ribbon bow or rosette.

Gustavian wall clock, signed J. Kock, with typical period detailing, including plumes, ribbon bows, laurel swags, urns, fleurons, and regular borders.

A Swedish gilded console-table with a curved, molded-edge limestone tabletop and carved decoration on the apron. Turned and fluted legs with an upper collar.

During the Rococo, mirror frames were almost always gilded, but it was only in 1767 that a "gilding commission" was instituted with the task of regulating gilders. In order to call oneself a master gilder and practice the craft, hopefuls had to spend five years as an apprentice, followed by five more as a journeyman, and before finally submitting to an examination. Those who flouted regulations risked a prison sentence. However, a mirror-maker could apply for special dispensation from the commission in order to silver and gild mirrors. On the whole, the craftsmen of the day were tightly controlled and subordinate to the master craftsmen, a system that in the eighteenth century resulted in furniture of the highest quality.

The pièce de résistance in any room

In the 1760s, the bureau or chest of drawers took over from the
cupboard as the most-prized masterpiece, the height of fashion, and the most important
form of storage furniture. While the Rococo was characterized by flowing lines,
the contours now became generally more austere, with straight sides and beveled
front corners, although High Gustavian and Late Gustavian styles
can be clearly distinguished from each other.

The High Gustavian bureau was richly
veneered in exotic woods, often in geometric patterns. The top of the chest of
drawers could be stone or limestone. The
master cabinet-makers had their own
patterns and templates, which became
their individual signatures. This bureau is
unsigned, but the intarsia with fruit bowl
and chessboard indicate the master cabinetmaker Gustav Foltiern, fl. 1771–1804. The
intarsia would earlier have been polychrome.

Left: The top of the bureau is a slab of molded-edge limestone with contours that follow the line of the bureau,
and beveled corners. The underside of the slab has tool marks from being cut by hand. The bronze fittings on
the middle panel are unusual, and consist of a beaded shield with laurel swags hanging from rings. The round
drawer pulls and keyhole plates surrounded by laurel wreaths are made of fire-gilded bronze.

Left: The uppermost drawer front is actually a folding flap for writing, hence the name "writing bureau" given to this type of bureau. Underneath the limestone slab is the name of the person who commissioned the piece in ink. Among the fittings are molded-brass medallions mounts. The lock is surface-mounted.

The Late Gustavian bureau is a mixture of French and English influences. From France come the restrained, rectilinear form and the three-drawer design. England contributed the undecorated mahogany veneer and the brass strips around the fronts of the drawers. Other typical details are the brass trim down the sides, the brass shoes on the legs, and the triangular struts that support the flap.

A Danish armchair with floral upholstery, an oval splat, and a round seat. The turned and fluted legs taper towards the feet.

The Late Gustavian sofa with its fixed, padded seat was built on classical lines with a rectangular padded back or, as here, an open back. The open armrests are padded. The floral decoration found on earlier sofas has now been replaced by a border in the form of a plaited ribbon carved along the apron, the back, and the armrests. The sofa legs have the same form as found on Gustavian chairs. The back ribs are leaf-capped below and are linked by elegant arches top and bottom, decorated with fleurons. The underside of the rear frame has the maker's seal and the signature, IEH, for Johan Erik Höglander, who was active in Stockholm in the period 1777–1813.

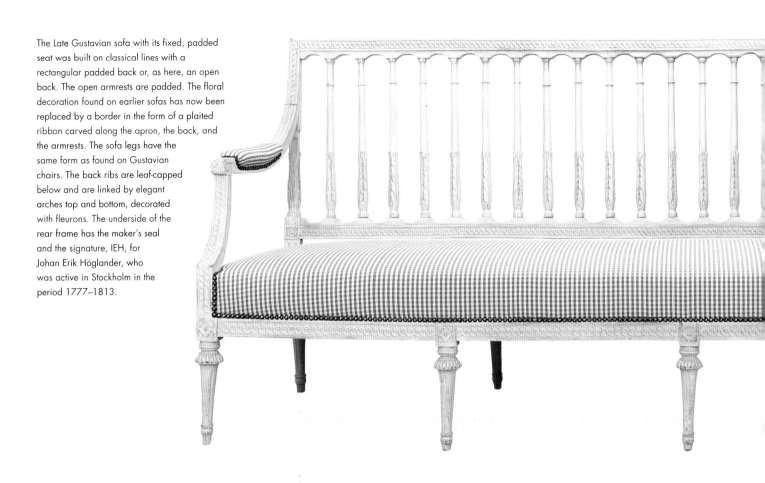

The need for increased comfort

During the Gustavian period many new forms of seating were developed, following trends from France and England. For the most part these consisted of sofas of varying lengths, chairs with and without armrests, and stools or tabourets. Sofas were unusually long, so that as many people as possible might sit on them. Later generations were often forced to get them shortened to fit their smaller rooms.

Gustavian chairs with a French pedigree had fully upholstered backs and a fixed padded seat. English-inspired variants were made with a removable seat resting on the frame and an open back with a splat or ribs of various designs. The most common colors for chairs were gold or various shades of grey, while Venetian red was used to imitate the more expensive mahogany.

A tabouret made in Stockholm with floral medallions wrapped round the blocks, an apron with a border of leaves, and fluted tapered legs.

Swedish chairs were a mixture of French and English influences: here the French is represented by the oval back and tapering legs, the English by the open back, the removable seat, and the turned H-stretcher. Carved fleurons blocks. Typical for this style of chair is the open baluster splat, a legacy from the slimmer Rococo style. The rail is decorated with a carved flower.

An open-back chair with three chain-shaped slats in the back. The legs and slats are fluted on the lower part and there is a turned H-stretcher. Fleurons on the blocks. Despite its simple lines, this is a superb example of work from Stockholm, signed AHM, for Anders Hellman, fl. 1793–1825.

English-inspired chair from the 1790s painted in Venetian red to resemble mahogany. The back consists of five turned bars with two heavier risers at the sides, which support a curved, molded rail. Turned, tapering legs connected by an H-stretcher. The tops of the legs have turned, molded buttons. The base of the back carries the signature ES, for Ephraim Ståhl, active in Stockholm 1794–1820.

An axstol, or wheat-sheaf chair, from western Sweden with fluted legs. The chair's name is derived from the carved wheat-sheaf decoration on the crest rail, and from the stylized form of the splat. The typical curved back, embellished by the five bound stalks of the splat, is taken from designs by the English cabinetmaker George Heppelwhite.

A chair from western Sweden with a beaded border with its original coloring, a rectangular back with wheat-sheaf splat, and tapered, fluted legs. Carved fleurons on the blocks. A unique detail is the carved beaded band along the apron and on the back.

Late Gustavian chair with a generous seat and a curved splat inspired by antique Roman "Sulla" models. Leaf border on the apron and back, and collared legs. The fleurons on the back harmonize with those on the blocks. The chair was made in Stockholm.

No chair made today
can compare to a Gustavian chair
from the eighteenth century.

Expert craftsmanship

To make a chair today according to the old traditions of craftsmanship would be exceedingly expensive. For the best durability, compact tight-grain wood was always used, often beech or birch. The inside of the hand-sawn frame shows the toolmarks of the saw-blade. The frame is mortised into the corner-blocks at the tops of the legs and fixed with a wooden dowel. The block is decorated with carved flowers—fleurons—on a burnished background. Other decorative elements are the regular, carved borders on the apron and the splat. The patina of the visible parts and the bare wood should match each other. If chairs from this period have been stabilized with extra corner-blocks the wood is usually of a different color. The seat stuffing is supported by webbing. The golden rule when renovating an antique chair is to proceed with caution at every step. Only replace wood that is essential for stability and durability. Many antique chairs are often repainted repeatedly, perhaps in inappropriate colors, which distracts focus from the decorative wood details. Never use chemical paint removers as they destroy the patina and damage the surface of the wood: Careful dry scraping is the preferred method.

A space to write, with a Gustavian chair and Nils Strinning's "String" shelving. The chair is French in influence with a trapezoidal back and fixed padding in the seat and back, upholstered in a finely striped red-and-white fabric. The apron and back are decorated with a carved border of leaves. The tops of the legs have overhanging gadrooning—a curved, concave–convex patterned band.

A dining area with a modern laminated table with stainless-steel legs. Around the table is a set of High Gustavian chairs in their original paint, upholstered in a grey-and-white striped fabric that sets off the oval backs with full-blown roses on their crests. A group of lit candles in a mixture of brass and silver-plate candlesticks create a striking focal point. Kartell's airy Bloom lamp above the table completes the look. A white bookcase in the Gustavian style is used for storage.

A rectangular writing-table in mahogany with a leather writing surface. At the back of the table is an array of pigeonholes and small drawers behind tambours—sliding flexible shutters. The brass fittings and details are typical of the Late Gustavian style.

A tilt-top table with alder-root veneer from the Mälaren Valley in central Sweden. The small tabletop can be locked in place. Typical construction with a turned pedestal supported on three feet. The table is signed "Jac: Siölin," for Jacob Sjölin, active in the town of Kungsör, 1767–1785.

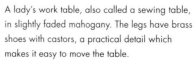

A lady's work table, also called a sewing table, in slightly faded mahogany. The legs have brass shoes with castors, a practical detail which makes it easy to move the table.

Tables for every purpose

During the Gustavian period there was an increase in the variety of types and sizes of tables, adapted to particular purposes around the home. Sweden's blooming social life meant that side tables were ever more important. The earliest tables were similar to the bureaus of the day in having intarsia decoration, while later models were mahogany with brass trim and saboted feet. It was at this time the tea table became popular. An inset faience tray prevented the wood surface from being damaged by the heat and damp when serving tea. The frame and legs were of mahogany and in the Gustavian idiom. Dining tables were made of pine, simple and undecorated. For celebrations they would be covered in beautiful damask tablecloths. When not in use they would be folded up and placed against the wall.

Rectangular side table with collared, fluted legs, painted at a later date. The apron and legs are decorated with a regular beaded border.

A striking juxtaposition of Arne Jacobsen's Egg chair in black leather and master cabinet-maker C.D. Fick's lady's work table in mahogany with brass details. Above the table hangs a gilded Late Gustavian mirror, by the mirror-maker Niklas Falkengren. Agneta Gynning's rubber statue "On my way" reinforces the contrast between the present and the past.

Long-case clock with restrained contours and a sweeping flared "skirt" with typical Gustavian embellishments: an urn at the top, regular egg-and-dart borders, and flanking pilasters with urns and pine cones. A laurel garland runs around the round glass window in the trunk. Another decorative element is the open book, which symbolizes knowledge. The clockface is enameled metal with brass hands and black, painted numbers, and has the clock-maker's name, Fredrik Bäckman, sometimes spelled Beckman. He was licensed to set up a clock-making business in 1786, and was active at his Gothenburg workshop until his death in 1819.

The bare brick wall is softened by the presence of a Gustavian long-case clock, a newly made, black-painted chair by Hans Wegner, and a modern floor-standing urn in glazed earthenware from China.

Lighting with sparkling mirrors and prisms

The ceiling-lights were airy chandeliers with diamond-ground or facetted prisms mounted on a slender ring of gilded bronze. The arms of the candleholders resemble a figure five laid on its side—a key detail in identifying Gustavian chandeliers. The prisms were not just elegant decoration; their primary function was to reflect the light. In the lower part of the chandelier there was a "welcome light," which was lit when entertaining in a style that did not require the main ring of candles to be lit.

Wall-mounted sconces were another light source. These were oval or rectangular mirrors with a candleholder in front. Girandoles were arrangements of candles on a pedestal foot with the upper part decorated with prisms to reflect the light. Mirrors on the walls were also used to enhance the lighting.

Carved and gilded rectangular mirror sconce with a pierced crest and bottom. A lit candle will give off a far stronger light in such a sconce. This particular sconce has new mirror glass.

A chandelier in the Gustavian style from the mid nineteenth century, with a bag of prisms at the bottom, a crown ring, and arms in the form of prostrate figure fives. Another key feature is the airy arrangement of diamond and facetted prisms. At the very bottom, the welcome light is burning.

A simple white sofa with matching footstool is complemented by a Gustavian armchair whose splat, with its carved rose on the crest rail, bears traces of the Rococo. The chair, by the Stockholm master chair-maker Carl Fredrik Flodin, is upholstered in a blue-and-white fabric that lightens the chair and the surrounding décor. The Chinese coffee table, with its open, latticed apron, enhances the lighting in the room. To the left of the sofa can be seen a commode in the Late Gustavian style in mahogany with brass detailing, signed by Erik Nyström. The durable limestone top makes the cupboard practical and useful even today. Another Gustavian touch is the pair of Swedish candlesticks with typical mahogany columns, beaded borders, gilded nozzles, and marble feet. A collection of nautical artifacts sets up a resonance with the sea beyond. Eighties Sweden is represented by floor lamps in plastic.

Hand-blown glasses with rounded funnel bowls, here decorated with an oak-leaf border, were a new fashion in Gustav III's day. The square, facetted foot is typical of the style. **Miniatures** were the photographs of the time, and were painted by skilled portraitists. This miniature has a gilded brass frame crowned by a rosette and ribbons and decorated with the beaded border so typical of the Gustavian era. This **mahogany casket** with ball feet and brass trim is a Late Gustavian piece that shows that the design principles were the same whatever the size of the object. The circular keyhole plate with laurel festoons is of a later date. **Reading lamp** with a green-painted adjustable metal screen, with a medallion-shaped marble base decorated with a seated dog in fire-gilded bronze.

A cylindrical silver coffee pot with regular beaded and leaf borders. The turned wooden handle, which is fitted at right angles to the pot, is finished with a bone knop. Made by Gustav Hamnqvist, who was active in the town of Åmal, 1789–1818.

Empire

An imperial and magnificent era with colorful
interiors, furniture in dark mahogany, and decoration
inspired by classical ideals.

Classical ideals in focus

The Empire style, a period characterized by fire-gilded bronze, is sometimes jokingly called the Second Bronze Age. The style developed in a politically unstable France at the end of the eighteenth century, at the time of the French Revolution and Napoleon's rise to power.

The leading architects and interior decorators of the Empire era were Charles Percier and Pierre Fontaine, who had both studied the classical antiquities in Rome during the 1780s. In 1801 they published a pattern book given over wholly to the new style. Their ideas were widely praised throughout Europe and Russia. In Britain the style went by the name of Regency style.

Napoleon helped to develop the style. His Egyptian campaign meant that Egyptian influences became fashionable. Several years later, once he had declared himself emperor, new luxurious elements drawn from the Roman Empire became part of the style.

The Empire style came to Sweden in 1810 with Jean Baptiste Bernadotte, one of Napoleon's marshals, who was elected king and took the name Karl XIV Johan. He introduced the French style by ordering furniture from France. The Swedish name for Empire style, "Karl Johan style," is named the first king of the House of Bernadotte.

The Empire style's visual form did not reflect the new France that was in the process of emerging. Quite the contrary. The interest in classical models that had inspired the previous, Gustavian style developed into a pure obsession. Everything had to be designed according to classical ideals, which were copied so slavishly that practicality and utility became of secondary importance.

The characteristic symbols of the style were many: griffins, sphinxes, lotus flowers, palmettes and palmette friezes, lyres, dolphins, and swans were just a few of the most common symbols. Warlike symbols included shields, helmets, and weapons. Nike, the winged goddess of victory, was another popular motif, as was Napoleon's own emblem, the eagle.

Sweden's so-called "Palace" Empire style was not as magnificent as its French archetype. The style, which in Sweden lasted until the middle of the nineteenth century, had a more unassuming and simple form, with a more bourgeois character.

A French faience cushion with the symbols of victory typical of the Empire style: the cup, the scepter, and wings. The boy, with victory wings and laurel wreath, is painted in Napoleon's likeness. A plaited band in gold runs around the cushion, which has faience tassels at each corner.

Wallpaper and colorful textiles

Wallpaper was introduced during the Empire period in the form of so-called panoramic or scenic wallpapers with painted scenes of classical ruins. Rooms were further decorated with objects such as table clocks, candlesticks, and urns in gilded or dark-patinated bronze or porphyry. Porphyry, a hard igneous rock that is difficult to work, had been used since ancient Egyptian times. It became fashionable again with the growing mania for classical antiquity.

The Empire style's grouping of furniture directly under a chandelier became the model for our current style of furnishing. Window curtains became a popular interior detail—preferably on a large scale and in strong colors such as lemon yellow, blue, green, red, or gold. In some extreme cases, a room would be entirely hung with textiles to resemble a Roman tent.

There is no clear dividing line between Late Gustavian furniture and pieces made in the Early Empire style. There was a transitional stage when furniture was often painted. Later, glossy polished mahogany became a favorite, decorated with gilt bronze or brass fittings to give the furniture a luxurious touch. Towards the end of the period, it became common for furniture to be made of birch.

Among the new forms of furniture to appear was the chiffonier, which usually stood on a plinth rather than legs. It had a double function, as it could be used for writing and for storage. Behind the fold-down flap was an array of small drawers and pigeonholes. In the finest examples the inside was built to resemble a Roman temple, complete with columns.

Empire chairs had splayed legs that swept backwards or forwards. Chair backs frequently terminated in a shield—a Greek pelta—with curved armrests and a fixed, padded seat. Other seating included the sofa (important for socializing), tabourets, and sofa benches—long stools fitted with armrests.

The Empire style's grouping of furniture directly under the chandelier became the model for our present style of furnishing.

Armchair in gilded wood with green-patinated details, probably by the royal chair-maker E. Ståhl, who worked in Stockholm. The dramatic backwards splay of the legs and the elegant final volute form of the back are examples of exquisite Swedish craftsmanship along classical lines. The chair is handsome enough to be placed on its own.

Mahogany, bronze, and porphyry

Tables took on increasing importance, and there was a growing interest in table decorations. Cookery books were published which included suggestions for table settings. Many different types of table were made, for example drop-leaf tables and sewing tables with lyre-shaped supports. Dining-tables could be round, consisting of two "demi-lune" semicircles in mahogany with tapered or tapered turning legs. The tabletop could often be extended with an extra leaf made of pine. A new style of table, the divan table, was introduced. It was usually made in mahogany with a single, central leg that might terminate in a gilded lion's paw. The tabletop was rectangular with folding flaps on the short sides, and sometimes a drawer in the apron.

The magnificent and richly decorated console table was usually mahogany or gilded. Both variants might have a stone top, perhaps held up by an eagle or a lyre. A new fashion was for a combination of a console table and a mirror or pier glass, called a trumeau after the architectural space it usually filled.

Empire-style mirrors had gilded or mahogany frames, flanked by two columns and with a straight or semicircular crest. The borders were carved wood or stucco.

Empire chandeliers were made using lightweight glass prisms on a metal frame. The crown ring became larger, and further candle-holders in playful designs were added, since there was a need for more brightly lit spaces. Sometimes the arms were shaped like dolphins. Hanging lamps based upon classical models were also popular, with a bowl and candleholders hanging on chains. Candela-bras were made from various materials, for example matt or glossy fire-gilded bronze, which could be combined with patinated bronze in dark hues, or with porphyry or marble. The many candleholders were held up on a bronze platter by classical figures of the victorious mold. Candlesticks were for the most part fire-gilded or plain brass. The reeded column was a usual shape, with a regular border around the foot with typical Empire symbols.

Many of the Empire clocks were made in France. They were often fire-gilded with elements in dark-patinated bronze. The actual clock-face was mounted in a built-up pedestal, decorated with Empire motifs.

The Empire style adopted motifs from the world of fable, both in basic construction and as decoration. The front of this mahogany console-table is held up by two long-necked swans with gilded feet and heads. This sort of furniture is easy to place as an occasional table in the hall, dining room, or sitting room.

Empire tables

The Empire period saw an increased demand for various types of table, and for a wider variety of surfaces for storage and display. The increasing importance of the sofa group led to the need for sofa tables. Among the bourgeoisie, small tables for sewing and embroidery became increasingly common. In the finest examples, the tabletop might be made of Swedish porphyry, white marble, or marbled wood. Birch and mahogany veneers were also used. The supports could take the form of a lyre, a winged eagle, or a shield. The console table was, as in other periods, a most exclusive item of furniture, often gilded, richly adorned, and preferably with a matching mirror.

This French table in mahogany has gilt metal fittings. It is constructed with a pillared base supporting an encased marble slab, with a drawer at the front. The oval mirror is flanked by two pillars, each terminating in a fire-gilded, chased knob.

A round sofa table in mahogany with an obelisk-shaped, triform foot. The wheels make it easy to move the table. A very useful occasional table for any hall or living-room.

A dining table in dark, glossy mahogany with well-chosen veneer forming a matching pattern. The table can be extended with additional table leaves. The tapered legs are a survival from the Gustavian era.

A divan table in mahogany, made in Stockholm. It is a so-called "drop-leaf" table that can be extended as needed by raising the flaps. The leg has been stained a darker color, and fitted with four carved and gilded lion's paw feet. The tabletop, with a drawer in the apron, has a gilded mount in the form of a lion mascaron or mask, behind which the keyhole is concealed.

Right: A new dining-table in high-gloss black paint complements the gilded Empire chairs, which have been upholstered in a modern fabric in black matt and gloss stripes. The chairs' green-patinated details include the lotus-capped legs and the stucco decoration of the apron. The upholstered, curved splat is pierced at the base. The period chandelier has typical Empire details such as the broad crown ring and dolphin-shaped arms.

Above: A mirrored ornamental tray or "plateau" with a fire-gilded bronze rim. The feet are Medusas, a favorite symbol from Roman mythology. The mirror quite literally forms a plateau, its role to reflect the table decorations and surroundings to enhance the overall effect of the setting. Today, a mirrored plateau can be used as a table decoration in place of the traditional vase of flowers.

A mahogany armchair with an upper rail
shaped like a pelta, or stylized Greek shield.
The support below is decorated with a brass
lotus flower. The seat of the chair has been
upholstered in a white fabric.

A typical Swedish mahogany chair with simple front and back legs. The airy back is decorated with a gilded oval laurel wreath, which indicates it was made in Stockholm. The damask-inspired upholstery in bright green is patterned with golden lyres.

A Russian mahogany Late Empire chair with gilded and carved details on the front legs and back. The broad splat is typical for Russian models. The legs are gently splayed.

Graceful, comfortable chairs

Empire chairs are easy to place and use, even in modern settings. Made in mahogany or less expensive birch, they are often graceful and inviting. Their saber legs are called for the weapon they resemble; their backs have soft contours.

A birch footstool, covered in practical black leather, which complements the wood well, and with the typical splayed legs of the Empire style. It would make a fine decorative piece in any room.

Swedish-made armchair in birch with typical shaped legs. The shape and decoration of the back support can vary. This chair has an oval decoration at the centre, decorated with a gilded oak leaf on a black ground.

Green paint was used
to imitate oxidation.

A smooth transition from the Late Gustavian to the Early Empire

A chair scraped back to its original grayish-white paint with retouched details in shades of green. The green paint was used to resemble oxidation or patina—everything was supposed to look as if it had just been dug out of the ground at a classical ruin.

The chair's lotus-capped, reeded front legs are straight and tapered. The back legs are square in section and sweep strongly backwards. The decoration on the blocks—where the legs meet the frame—and the regular borders is made from stucco, a mixture of hide glue, plaster, chalk, and linseed oil. The centre part of the splat is a made up of carved leaves.

Empire details include the Egyptian female figures holding up the rectangular upholstered rail. The stucco fleurons on the blocks and the lotus-capped legs are painted green to give an impression of patina. The chair is a good example of quality furniture made for stately homes.

The essential sofa

The sofa took a vital position in Empire salons, where the idea of a sofa group
in combination with a sofa table was introduced. Sofas were usually
in mahogany with a fixed, padded back. The other seating in the salon
could be upholstered in the same material as the sofa.

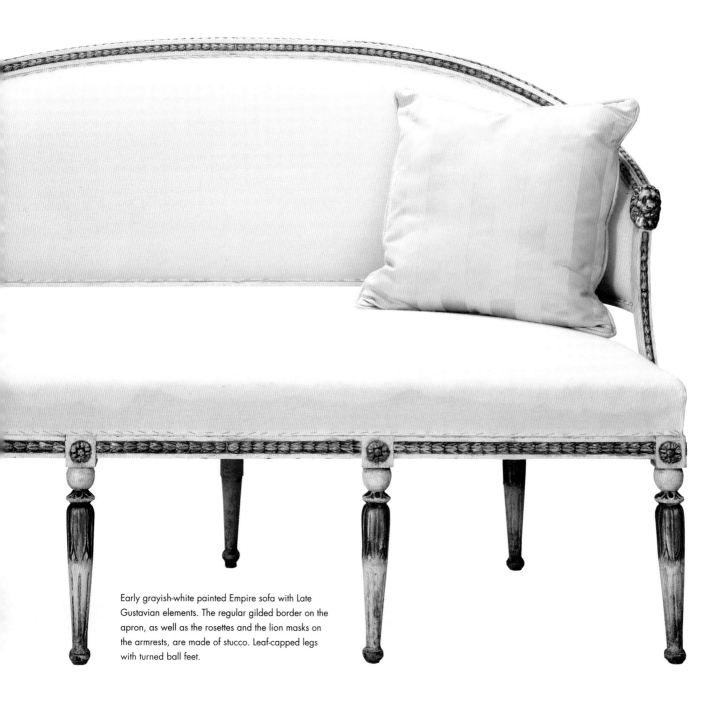

Early grayish-white painted Empire sofa with Late
Gustavian elements. The regular gilded border on the
apron, as well as the rosettes and the lion masks on
the armrests, are made of stucco. Leaf-capped legs
with turned ball feet.

A French Empire sofa upholstered in black leather with a decorative border of tacks and gilt bronze mounts. The armrests have a soft form and the shaped legs are fitted with gilded lion's paw feet. A hardwearing piece of furniture that would be easy to find a home for.

This austere, modern space includes a seating area with an early Swedish Empire sofa with an open back and sides. Modern loose cushions in neutral grey velvet increase the sofa's comfort and accentuate its beautiful shape. Another antique piece is the chiffonier in dark, polished mahogany with gilt bronze fittings. Upon it stand two Empire candlesticks and a pair of tazzas—shallow ornamental dishes—from the same period.

The endpieces of the sofa have been scraped back to the original paint and have stucco decorations of two small sphinxes with a palmette in between. The sofa is a clear example of the transition between the Late Gustavian and Early Empire styles.

Above: The gilt bronze lion mascarons with the rings of the drawer pulls in their jaws are a typical Empire detail. In the centre of the leather-clad flap is a symbolic North Star. The edge of the inset leather top insert has embossed and gilded details. The brass lock is surface mounted, which means it is visible on the inside of the flap. The chiffonier's legs terminate in feet in the form of carved and gilded lion's paws.

Left: A French chiffonier in glossy, polished mahogany. The straight flap has a leather writing surface. Inside the flap are small drawers and pigeonholes.

Above: A Swedish **urn in porphyry** that would have been filled with pot-pourri to help make the salon smell more pleasant. Porphyry was an important element in Sweden's cultural heritage. For several years, King Karl XIV Johan himself owned the Elfdahl porphyry works. The lid's pine cone knop is of fire-gilded bronze.

Left: On the round birch-wood table are a selection of Empire *objets*: a French **table clock** in fire-gilded and patinated bronze with Apollo playing his lyre; **a pair of candlesticks**, again in gilded and patinated bronze, both on tripod feet with lion's paw feet; a Swedish-made **alder-root casket** in the form of a sarcophagus; a **paperweight** in red marble with a gilded snake; and a **snuffbox** made of masur birch in the shape of a dog with a brass collar.

Gilded mirrors and glittering chandeliers

Mirrors symbolized not vanity, but truth and wisdom. They were regarded as the shining face of godly power. In the Empire period, tall, thin, wall-mounted mirrors with a matching console-table became common in mansions and stately homes.

Chandeliers became even more important as people wanted more light for their festivities. The Late Gustavian form lived on, but the crown became heavier and had more arms, which took on more imaginative shapes, often in the form of swans or dolphins. Hanging lamps in gilded and patinated bronze were another common form of lighting.

A mirror with matching console-table. This mirror with its flanking stylized fasces is signed C.F.G. for Carl Gustaf Fyrwal, a mirror-maker from Stockholm. The crest is a semicircular "lunette," and is framed by a stucco border with a palmette motif. The console table's top of white Carrara marble is attached directly to the wall. The pierced volute form of the legs is decorated with leaves. The edge the table and lunette frame of the mirror have matching decoration.

Rings of icicle prisms forming the waterfall at the base of a chandelier—an innovation of the Empire period. At the very bottom is a holder for a single candle for when it was not necessary to light the entire chandelier.

A round Swedish **sugar bowl**, with fluted decoration and a leaf handle, standing on a base with lion's paw feet. Because sugar was a luxury, the sugar bowl is a casket with a lock to keep out prying fingers. A **cream jug** on a tripod foot with a swan pedestal. The gadrooned body is gilded on the inside. **Teapot** in a bulging form with a molded oval foot. The elongated spout ends in a horse's head, and a squirrel is sitting eating nuts on the lid. The practical handle in stained wood does not get hot. A cylinder-shaped **mustard pot** with a blue glass insert that prevents the mustard from corroding the silver. The pot has a volute-shaped loop handle and small molded feet.

Embossed silver lyre candlesticks from Möllenborg's workshop in Stockholm. The sinuous decoration of the foot and candleholder are signs of the transition to the Revivalist style.

Folk Art

The Folk Art style, with its simple furniture
and brilliantly colored textiles made by
Sweden's countryfolk.

Country furniture

Sweden's *Allmogen*, "Everyman's style," is the Folk Art style of peasant furniture and culture that ran from the second half of the eighteenth century to the mid nineteenth century. The inspiration for Folk Art furniture was taken from furnishings of the salons of the wealthy, but it took a long time for their influence to be felt in farming communities, and they were simplified in the process to better suit their rural setting. The wood used for furniture was usually pine, but birch was not unknown.

Folk Art furniture was produced by local carpenters and painters whose main livelihood was often something quite different—the army, say, or farming. Furniture-making was a way for smallholders and soldiers to eke out their income during the long winter months when there was little do on the land. These "hobby craftsmen" did not have to belong to a carpenter's guild of any kind, something that was compulsory in the larger towns. This is why Folk Art craftsmen can be so difficult to trace and identify. On the other hand, it is possible to tell where in Sweden Folk Art furniture comes from, because its form, color, and decoration is full of local characteristics. A greenish-blue ground thus points to the southern part of the country, while a darker shade indicates a central Swedish origin. Furniture from northern Sweden is distinguished by its use of lighter blue paint. Most highly rated today is Folk Art furniture painted in several different colors—polychrome—and still with its original paint.

A farmhouse would have been furnished with a few pieces functional furniture, each with its given place in the living room. A large press-cupboard, a so-called *salsskåp*, usually stood to the right of the door as one entered. There might also be a wall-mounted "wall-cupboard" where the master of the house kept the household's liquor, snuffbox, and other small possessions. The long-case clock would have stood opposite the door, the first thing visitors would see as they entered the room.

Seating consisted of benches fixed along the walls along with a few chairs or stools. The table was usually a trestle-table, the board laid on a pair of trestles that were stabilized with wedged crossbars. After the 1870s, farmers began to furnish their homes in much the same style as middle-class townsfolk. Upholstered hardwood furniture became more common, and the sofa and chairs were grouped under the chandelier.

Sofa bed in Swedish "gentry joinery," decoratively carved in the Gustavian idiom. The new cushion is a modern copy in cotton of an old tapestry-woven carriage cushion from the county of Skåne.

The finest textiles were stored in large chests,
to be brought out for Easter, Christmas, weddings,
and other special occasions.

What brightened farming families' lives were their painted
cupboards, chests, and caskets, and their textiles and tapestries.
Textiles were produced at home by the women of the household,
and were thought of as farmers' gold. Folk Art box-beds were
cheered up with brightly colored bolsters and quilts. Just like the
furniture, Folk Art textiles display clear geographical differences
in motif, weave, and choice of natural dyes. The southernmost
county of Skåne was known for its colorful wool embroideries
of geometric patterns of lozenges and stars, above all used for
carriage cushions and seat cushions, and for its tapestry-woven
fabrics with patterns in the shape of urns. The southern coun-
ties of Blekinge and Halland were known for their narrow,
white *hängkläden*, or wall-hangings, embroidered in vibrant
red tones. Bed textiles from the north of Sweden were characterized by their white ground with embroidered borders in bril-
liant colors. The finest textiles were stored in large chests, to be
brought out for Easter, Christmas, weddings, and other special
occasions.

Chests were the commonest forms of storage, and were often
associated with weddings. If a bride had a well-filled chest to
show for her dowry, it gave her considerable standing in the
eyes of the community. Bridal chests often bear two sets of
initials and the year of the marriage.

The smaller caskets were used to store items of a more personal nature, such as letters, jewelry, and other small valuables.
It was not unusual for a casket to be given as a gift to mark a
betrothal or a wedding.

Swedish wedding press-cupboard or *ståndsskåp*, with
panels of painted flowers in marbled frames, and two
pairs of initials and the year. There is a bottom drawer
the width of the cupboard. An excellent piece of storage
furniture to this day.

Kurbits, the richly painted floral motifs
for which the county of Dalarna was known,
is a stylized explosion
of fantastical flowers and foliage.

Art for Folk Art's sake

A southern Swedish **Folk Art chest** dated 1846. The chest bears the owner's initials, surrounded by exuberant polychrome tulips and flowers. The lid is decorated with two painted flower urns. The chest would work as a coffee table in the living-room or as a useful place to put things down in the hall. Or why not a bedside table to store bulky bedding?

Hanging **corner-cupboard** dated 1797, with initials and painted "kurbits" decoration. Kurbits, the richly painted floral motifs for which the county of Dalarna was known, is a stylized explosion of fantastical flowers and foliage. Small wall-cupboards often turn up at auction these days. With their painted decoration, many of them are beautiful works of art.

An oval **gate-legged table** with two rounded table leaves. Chairs by Leksandsstolen with a molded spindle back and straight, plain legs reinforced with stretchers. The nineteenth-century chandelier has a turned wooden baluster, shaped arms, and metal nozzles. The tea service is Stig Lindberg's classic "Berså."

Shaving mirror box in wood, clad in fabric painted to resemble wood. The inside is lined with green cotton, and has drawers for shaving kit and writing materials. The small ink bottles go with the box.

Folk Art casket, the body made of thin strips of wrapped wood and painted with flowers. To strengthen it, it has hand-wrought iron edging and details.

Go confidently
in the direction
of your dreams!
Live the life
you've imagined.
-Thoreau

An old, patinated pine table with an
untreated top and a drawer in the apron
now serves as a desk, with a Swedish swivel
chair in birch. The seat cushion in blue-and-
white striped cotton is a modern copy of an
old Swedish original. An old step-ladder
has found a new home as a bookshelf and
magazine rack.

Revivalism

Styles from earlier periods remade in the spirit
of a new age, with dark woods, saturated colors,
and a wealth of textiles.

New versions of old styles

Revivalism is an umbrella term for a variety of decorative styles found in Europe in the period 1830–1895. All share an origin in a nostalgic desire for a more decorated, exotic architecture. The different varieties of Revivalism took their forms and symbols from earlier styles such as the Renaissance, Baroque, Rococo, and Louis XVI, all of which provided important inspiration. However, in the Revivalist version there was a change of materials and an evolution of the style, which acquired an even more exaggerated decorative sense than the original. The Revivalist styles are not fashionable now, but the furniture produced is of good craftsmanship, is comfortable to use, and is well built in excellent materials.

Industrialization in the mid nineteenth century brought with it a revolution in interior design and furniture-making. Suddenly it became possible to mass-produce furniture at low cost. The old esteem in which furniture of past ages was held now disappeared: Most people preferred new furniture, and for the bourgeoisie it was important to furnish and decorate their homes in a way that demonstrated that they were in step with the dictates of fashion.

The earliest forms of Revivalism were Gothic Revival and Baroque Revival. They won much popularity in Britain, but did not reach the same heights in Sweden; instead, the movement that enjoyed the greatest popularity in Continental Europe was Rococo Revival. The period is sometimes called the Age of Passementerie for its enthusiasm for draperies, carpets, and curtains, all embellished with passements—elaborate fringes, tufts, and tassels.

During the 1830s, the new French royal family came to serve as a model for the style, which reached Sweden in the 1840s and remained popular for the remainder of the nineteenth century. Neo-Rococo was in fact its own unique style, despite borrowing its sweeping curves from the Rococo proper. What most of all distinguished the Rococo Revival from the original, eighteenth-century Rococo was the choice of wood: Neo-Rococo furniture was made from solid, polished hardwoods such as mahogany and walnut. The chairs, too, differed from the originals: the point where the apron met the leg was given a stronger S-form, while the backs and rails took on exaggerated shapes and decoration. Another novelty was in the construction of the seats. Spiral springs held in place with webbing were introduced, which gave the seat a swollen look—and greater comfort.

A mixture of English Rococo Revival silver-plate candlesticks and modern Swedish glass.

Before an open fire stand two comfortable English wingback armchairs, covered in distressed leather, with brass furniture tacks highlighting their contours. The modern teak tray table creates an interesting contrast with the armchairs' voluminous presence. On the Swedish green marble mantelpiece are an African mask from the nineteenth century and three Ming dynasty pots.

Revivalist forms
and motifs had their roots
in earlier periods.

Furniture and objects to use

A French **occasional table** in mahogany in the Neo-Gustavian style. It is decorated with bronze detailing in the form of a grille along the edge and filled reeded legs. The top is made of practical cream-and-tan marble. This table does not take up much space and would fit in well in most modern homes.

A Neo-Rococo upholstered **slipper chair** was called an "emma" in Sweden: especially popular was a back with deeply set buttons, a so-called tufted back. Emmas were, and still are, very comfortable and easy to integrate into modern settings.

A Rococo Revival **shaving mirror** in walnut on a spiral-turned pedestal with a tripod foot. The table has with a drawer for toiletries. The oval mirror, swung on its frame, has carved decoration on the crest.

Imagine being served coffee from this attractive **porcelain set** from Germany in white and gold, with its coffee pot, cream jug, and sugar bowl, all in the Neo-Rococo style. Coffee services, which were a novelty in the nineteenth century, are still eminently usable—perhaps instead of a coffee-maker to give your day that little something extra.

An armchair in the Baroque style from the end of the nineteenth century, recently painted black. The seat has been fitted with an extra cushion for extra comfort. Upholstered in a modern black-and-white material, with diagonal stripe piping. The armrests end in deeply carved acanthus leaves with strong patina. In the background is Mats Theselius's yellow National Geographic cupboard from 1990.

Practical advice

Advice and inspiration for anyone interested in
furnishing their home with antiques.

From the left:
The detail of a Swedish Empire mirror from the first half of the nineteenth century, showing the beautiful decoration on the crest.

Close up of the clockface of a Gustavian long-case clock. The enameled clockface has brass hands and black, painted numbers.

Beautiful wood carving in the shape of fluted grooves on the front stile of a Gustavian sofa.

A brass hinge on a Late Gustavian bureau.

What to bear in mind when buying antiques

An antique is an object or a piece of furniture that is usually more than an hundred years old. Its value can be judged from two different perspectives: cultural and economic.

The cultural worth of a piece will include its history, for without history, there is no space for a meaningful present or future. Sentimental value is another dimension to this: Objects from a bygone age have a special character that is important for many people. Old things and modern design can enrich one another and set up exciting dialogues—and are a way of re-using the old instead of just chasing the new.

In other words, buying with your heart as well as your head is never wrong. Your own feelings for an object are something that should be taken into account. That said, there are a few questions well worth asking yourself before you decide. Where, for example, are you going to put the antique? Does it have to be of practical use, or is it simply for decoration?

A polished oak chest, somewhat smaller than its original form. It can be used as a seat, as an occasional table or a coffee table, or for storage.

All sizes and shapes. Here, a hand-carved toy horse from the end of the nineteenth century is happily stabled under a modern nesting table.

Think things through carefully before you decide to buy. The financial value of antiques depends upon their quality and age. It is impossible to give a precise valuation for an antique object, or to predict its future value, no matter how much experience and knowledge you have. The best choices are objects in their original state from the various styles before 1850, especially if their provenance can proved with a signature or stamp—that would bode well for the object's resale value.

Antiques may be bought at auction, at an antique shop, or online. If you prefer auctions, you need to know what you are doing.

Expect there to be additional costs for any renovation work that needs to be done. If you choose to go to an antique shop or dealer, make sure they are a bona fide business and that they offer professional help and advice. Membership of a professional association is a good indicator of quality. Also, dealers often have antiques that have already been restored, and which you can even have at home before deciding to buy.

The more you know about antiques, the more fun it is. The world of antiques is an exciting one, combining beautiful objects, history, architecture, and craftsmanship. And

A pair of French tazzas in marble with dark-patinated and gilded bronze makes useful decorative details on a bureau in the hall or on a windowsill.

A Swedish card table from the eighteenth century, with split and flaking paint. Dry scraping and perhaps a touch up with paint could restore the table to a beautiful condition.

all antiques have a story to tell, for those who care to listen.

Back to the future

How you like your antiques is a question of taste. Perhaps you like retaining all the layers of paint that have been added down the centuries and which are part of the furniture's invisible history. Or you may be curious about what is hidden under that topmost layer of white paint and want to recreate the original look. Whichever you choose, there is no wrong answer, provided the furniture is brought to life. To return a piece of furniture to its original condition, the preferred method is careful dry scraping; it is a time-consuming process, but it gives the best results. If dry scraping does not make the surface of the furniture more pleasing, the surface can be retouched with paint. Try to recreate the original colors of the furniture, and so realize the intentions of the maker.

Damaged wood or other problems should be put right so that the furniture can be used and will last longer. The golden rule is to replace as little as possible. If you are uncertain, consult a professional furniture restorer.

Gustavian armchair of the
"Swedish" model with a
pierced baluster splat.

Rococo chairs from western Sweden upholstered in a patinated brandy-colored leather. A good choice of durable material.

One variant on an upholstered back for an eighteenth-century chair.

Upholster to taste

Leather or textiles—when it comes to reupholstering antique seating, personal taste comes to the fore. It is never wrong to cover an antique chair or sofa in a modern or strongly colored fabric; just make sure that the seat is reasonably comfortable and has proper support. The most important thing is to not do anything you are unhappy about. You can always consult a professional for help. Before re-covering you should check that the basic upholstery is in good condition. A much-used seat often sags in the middle, and cannot offer the same degree of comfort as a firmer support would do. The height and depth of the seat are important factors to consider. When seated, the front edge of the seat should be just behind your knees. Choose upholstery fabric that you like. Bear in mind, however, that heavier, stronger materials hold their shape better and last longer. A heavy, tightly woven fabric will also be better at filling out any small defects in the stuffing often found on older chairs.

Stately English candelabras
in silver plate from the mid
nineteenth century. The arms
are cornucopias, a symbol of fertility
much used inthe Empire period. The
candelabras can be divided and used
as candlesticks.

Creating interiors with antique and modern furnishings

Antiques should work as part of everyday life; they should not be treated as museum objects. You should be able to use them—you should be able to sit on your antique sofa.

Start from your existing furniture and style, and try to find antiques that enhance your home and create contrasts. A Rococo bureau can bring a restrained modern setting to life.

Attempt to strike a balance between antiques and modern furniture so that the overall impression does not become too busy. Avoid having too many antiques in a room. One object, or a pair, will have a far greater effect. If you already have a lot of antiques, consider grouping them to create a calmer effect.

Do not be afraid to let rip with modern fabrics when reupholstering an antique chair or sofa. You can create coherence by using textiles of similar types and color scales for all your chairs and sofas. It brings calm and harmony to a room.

Try using leather too—it fits in well with most forms of seating, from the Baroque to the Empire style, plus it is durable and can easily cope with a grubby toddler or a splash of wine.

Mahogany furniture is undervalued, both when it comes to quality and price. It adds elegance to a room and fits in when combined with lighter woods or painted furniture.

Antique mirrors provide beautiful details that can enlarge, open up, and give depth to a room. Antique candlesticks, candelabras, and chandeliers are fabulous mood-setters that add an extra dimension.

It is the small details that make the whole thing work. Candlesticks, casket, porcelain, and silver are good examples of objects that can only enhance a room.

Including antiques in your home is a way of caring for the treasures of the past and the craftsmanship they embody.

Glossary

acanthus, decorative representation of the laciniated leaves of acanthus

applique, wall-mounted light with one or more arms

apron, the wooden sides of a table or chair to which the legs are attached and which forms a frame for the seat

argent haché, silver-plated brass

B

baluster, slender column or support that swells to a pear-shaped bulge at the bottom

block, carved decoration at the joints of the apron

C

cabinet, a richly decorated cupboard with two doors and an interior array of many small drawers and pigeonholes

cabriole legs, furniture legs which curve outwards from the frame and inwards at the foot

candelabra, a large candlestick with two or more candles on separate arms

cavetto, a concave rounded molding often found on furniture legs

C-form, see volute

chasing, embossed surface, engraved in relief

collar, shaped, overhanging band common on furniture legs

column, a cylindrical weight-bearing support divided between base and capital

console table, a small semi-circular or rectangular table, placed against or directly mounted on a wall

creamware, an alternative to porcelain launched in England in 1762

crown ring, the metal ring of a chandelier to which the arms are fixed

D

divan table, round or oval drop-leaf sofa table with a pedestal leg

dovetailing, a joint between two pieces of wood with interlocking wedges

E

egg-and-dart border, border with regular, stylized oval forms

F

faience, earthenware with a tin glaze

fleuron, decorative lozenge or knob in the shape of a flower

flutes, parallel concave grooves on a column

G

gesso, a mixture of chalk and diluted hide glue used to prepare surfaces for painting or gilding

gilt leather, embossed leather with painted decoration and gold or silver leaf

griffin, mythological animal with the head and wings of an eagle and the body of a lion

H

H-stretcher, 'H'-shaped reinforcing between the legs of a table or chair

I

intarsia, an arrangement of thin pieces of different types of wood glued to a support to create pictures and patterns

L

laurel swag, a festoon or rope of laurel leaves hanging between two holders

leaf-capped, carved representation of lotus at the top of a leg

lotus flower, a flower ornament from East Asian and Egyptian art

lunette, a semi-circular field

M

mascaron, a mask, a stylized face or animal head

N

night table, a casket or small chest for toiletries or minor items of clothing

O

obelisk, a tall, tapering stone pillar

P

pagoda, a type of traditional Buddhist temple in China and Japan

palmette, a decorative element formed by a stylized palm frond or palm tree

panorama wallpaper, a paper wall covering with pictures such as landscapes, mythological cities, and hunting scenes.

papier mâché, paper mass mixed with glue

patina, the surface coating, corrosion, or coloration that appears as an object ages

patinate, to create a patina by artificial means.

pelta, the name for a Greek or Roman shield, reminiscent of a crescent moon

poliment, or bole, a red undercoat used to prepare wood surfaces for gilding

polychrome, many-colored porphyry, a dense, hard igneous rock with large crystals of feldspar

porphyry, a dense, hard igneous rock with large crystals of feldspar

putto, representation of a naked baby, usually a boy, with or without wings.

R

reeds, parallel convex grooves on a column

reflector, a glossy or reflecting surface used to spread and increase the light from candles

retouching, improving appearance

ribbon bows, rosettes with trailing ribbons

rocaille, an asymmetric shell-like ornament built up of C and S curves

S

sconce, wall-mounted bracket-candlestick with one or more arms

S-form, see volute

sofa bench, padded stool or bench with low armrests

sphinx, a mythological animal with a human head on the body of a lion

spring lock, a lock which includes a spring to drive the bolt back and forth

still life, a group of objects

stucco, a mixture of chalk, plaster, hide glue, and linseed oil used to create relief ornament and borders

sulla, a chair with a broad crosspiece on the back and splayed legs

T

tabouret, a stool or low seat with no back or armrests

tazza, shallow ornamental dish, usually supported on one foot

tripod, three-legged

tufted back, upholstery fixed with deep-set buttons to prevent the stuffing from slipping

V

veneer, thin slices of fine wood glued to cover coarser wood

volute, C- or S-shaped ornamentation in a spiral form

vril, a burl or burr, usually birch or masur birch, hollowed out to make a bowl

W

webbing, a coarse, woven broad strap used to make of chairs, sofas, and beds

Carolean armchair in dark-stained,
polished oak and birch upholstered in
black velvet. Comfortable and useful in
the modern home.